REFLECTIONS
IN A
BRASS HELMET

On December 4th. 1904 at a celebration evening held in the new Hitchin Fire Station at Paynes Park, the following statement was made by C.L. Barham the brigade second officer, "Perhaps Mr. Logsdon (the Chief Fire Officer) will some day unfold the tale of the development of the Brigade from Isaac Newtons days to the present time. A list of fires from Brigade records and the names of firemen with their dates of service would be of much interest".

Before I had set eyes on this statement, I had completed a short history of the Brigade, encompassed in 4 wall plaques and hung in the new fire station at Newtons Way.

These aroused a great deal of interest, and as small errors with dates and additional information kept coming to light, rather than do the plaques again I consider writing a small book.

When I read Barhams statement it convinced me, that a book, although of limited interest, would at least be a record of the Hitchin Fire Brigade.

Brigade history is infact reasonably well documented by Reginald Hine up to 1929, and in some respects I have just reworded information that he researched. From 1929 onwards, to my knowledge, nothing has been recorded in depth and to that end, through a firemans eyes, I have endeavoured to put this to right.

This book is for all Hitchin Firemen, Past~Present & Future.

Acknowledgments

When I first thought of compiling an up to date complete History of Hitchins' Fire Brigade, I was disappointed to find many records missing. My main source in the beginning was Reginald Hines History of Hitchin. I then began to delve deeper into the Brigade log books and newspaper records at Hitchin Museum. My grateful thanks to Mr. Alan Fleck & his staff for all their help so willingly given.

I found that much of Hines' information relied on C.L. Barhams record of the time, who was the brigade secretary. I was later fortunate to receive from Mr Geoffrey Grant, the son of Walter Grant (a later Brigade Secretary) the very records and diary of C.L.Barham jnr. plus many very interesting documents, letters and photographs.

Sadly Geoffrey Grant has since died.

For the war records and later I have relied on news-paper cuttings and information from some of the 'old hands' — Henry Terry, Alf Whittenbury, John Gatward, Des. Huthwaite, Frank Symons, Ernie Reynolds; also Mr. Derek Wheeler and many others, who have volunteered pieces of information, and if I have left anyone out, it is only because to include them all would take as long as the book itself. My grateful thanks to them all.

My main aim in writing this book has been to put the History of Hitchins' Fire Brigade into one complete document. Hopefully this will be only a beginning and somebody in the future will carry on this task.

Finally I apologize in advance for any grammatical and spelling errors in this my first book.

D.B.Dolan 1989

~ Chapter ~
~ ONE ~

In 1189 Richard I passed laws that obliged the Lord Mayor of London to ensure that,~ Party walls should be installed between houses, and ladders were to be positioned outside houses to assist neighbours in the case of fire. Pits were to be dug for water supplies and a good horn supplied for the Beadle~This act was supplemented in 1285, ordering all villages to employ a watchman. Thus the small market town of Hitchin gained a watchman, whose task was to alarm the towns' people by crying, "Fire, Fire, keep in your beds!"

1666 saw the Great Fire of London and it is not hard to understand the fear felt by many local people after watching the clouds of smoke during the day and the crimson glow in the sky at night. When riders came from London demanding help, Hertfordshire responded by sending 200 soldiers, 6 of which came from Hitchin. Sent to London with pickaxes & spades, the six men are reported never to have returned. It would be nice to think that perhaps at least one of these men returned, with stories of horrific events and tales of gallant deeds, to be exaggerated every time the story was told. (Something that still happens in Fire Brigade circles today.)

The churchwardens were certainly concerned, as their firefighting equipment extended to a number of 20 foot fire hooks, and a few leather buckets. When in use the hooks were secured by ropes to teams of men or horses, to drag burning buildings down, to save adjacent buildings.

The news of the devastation from London and various laws following on after 1666, called upon the churchwardens to make provisions for, "Engines, Fire cocks & leather pipes". They purchased their first small engine in the late 17th. century. A very simple machine, a cistern of oak on four solid wheels, one foot in diameter, an 8 foot long reservoir, 2 foot wide & 18 inches deep. Having a brass pump in the centre with a swivel branch on the top. This pumping engine was stored in St. Marys Church tower along with the leather buckets & fire hooks. This old pump ended its days as a water trough in the cattle market.

In 1683, Wm. Hale of Kings Walden started an organisation, which along with others was to influence the brigade for 250 years. Hale started an insurance scheme, calling it a Friendly Society. In 1685 members were asked to pay their part of the fees; 5 shillings & 1 penny in respect of a loss of £695 incurred at a fire where seven house were destroyed by fire.

In 1707 a further edict was announced by the government of Queen Anne, establishing the responsibility for firefighting firmly on the churchwardens. This is reflected in an example of the churchwardens accounts, where in April 1717, £7~8s~0d. was paid for "four dozen buckets" inclusive of 4/- carraige and one shilling and sixpence for a man to hang up the buckets.

In 1722 the wardens purchased a further two engines, one at £14, and the other at £8, the old one was sold for £6. In 1730 David Marshall, a churchwarden, was dispatched to London to purchase a third engine from Mr Deane at a cost of £30~15s~0d. The town was now in possession of 3 engines, a considerable achievement for a small town at that time.

The Beadle
(principle fireman)
&
The Watchman
(with lamp & rattle)

An Early Manual Engine

W hen "Fire" was called in the 18th. century, men would rush to the church, there to manhandle the pumps to the scene of the fire, or to load them onto wagons if the fire was at one of the Hamlets, such as Walsworth. There was never a shortage of volunteers to "Play the engine", as they were supplied with free beer for their efforts. In some cases if beer did not materialise, the building was left to burn. Never the less on most occasions the beer flowed freely, in some cases reportedly, more beer flowed than water! At a fire at Luton Hoo, 14 gallons of beer was drunk and 11 shilling & 5 pennies worth of bread & cheese was consumed. One vicar of St Marys even built a brewery in the churchyard!

This was the status of the towns fire brigade in the 18th. century. The result of fire, accentuated by the lack of equipment in those days, was so destructive, it is worth mentioning some notable fires which indicate how helpless and inadequate the Brigade and the equipment was, especially to calls outside of the towns curtilage. In 1737 Stagenhoe House was destroyed by fire. In 1783 Hitchin experienced 13 fires in 20 weeks, all due to incendriarism ÷ October 21st. the kiln house of Mr. Lyle, at New England was fired, as was Mr Burys maltkiln in Tilehouse

The Hale Family Coat of Arms

street on the 31 st; Collisons barn in Butts Close in November and Sam: Lucas Cost his chaff house on the same night. Calls to Willian, Gosmore, and Maidencroft were experienced. The arson attacks were to continue into 1784.

Mr. Radcliffe offered a £50 reward and a Kings pardon to the accomplices, for the arrest of the offender. The Hertfordshire society for the security of property, made a more comprehensive policy. One of its clauses offered £10 "on conviction of the act of maliciously and wilfully destroying buildings and property".

Finally a first mention of firemen, where in 1771, R. Baker, Wm: Ball, John Day, John Jeeves, Ben Munsley, Wm: Smith and Francis Field, were paid for work done at "Widow Hawks fire".

The church was the focal point of the community and had considerable influence. When the church read the BRIEFS on Sundays the congregation and towns people were being asked to give money, which would go to people or other towns who had suffered through tragedy or disaster. More often than not the cause being fire. The King in 1660 "advised" the churches to read these briefs, but they had been used for some considerable time, as early as 1598, where Tiverton in Devon suffered damage estimated at £150000 due to fire. 50 persons burned to death and 940 people lost everything. A case more local was that of BRIDGET ANSELL of Cadwell farm, Ickleford, who sustained a loss of £137 due to a vagrant setting light to her barns. "Widow Ansell was granted license to take charitable benevolence of well disposed persons in the county of Hertfordshire."

Between 1663~1730 St. Marys Church, Hitchin read 350 BRIEFS

In 1814 from within the ranks of the churchwardens a certain Robert Newton emerged as a leading light for the Hitchin Fire establishment. His family ties go back 200 years to his business establishment in Tilehouse street. His occupation, builder, plumber & glazier. He suggested that he could accomodate the small fire engines and equipment at present in St Marys church, in his works yard. One assumes the vicar of St. Marys and the churchwardens, whose responsibilities were growing, welcomed the idea. He inaugurated a committee of towns people, namely Wm. Hawkins, G. Groom, R. Tatham, H. Cannon, J. Newton, A. Marshall, J. Ransom, Septimus Wright, (treasurer), Maning, W. Hainworth, T. Lowden, J. Peirson, Wm. Langford, Wm. Lucas, and representatives of the insurance agents. With these people he con- vinced the rate payers to pay for a larger engine, a Bristow & son, 20 man manual pump. Purchased in 1815, it had 6 inch piston barrels with 6½ inch strokes. (This engine was later to run over Fireman Dawbun, with tragic results, en-route to a fire at Weston.)

St Marys Church.

Robert Newton placed his son Isaac, aged 29 years in charge of the Brigade and gave him the title of Superintendent. Supt. Newton with 24 picked and trusted brigadiers as they were called, were the first indications of a disciplined force that could be called FIREMEN. Isaac certainly had his fathers ways, as in 1834 he pushed the rate payers once again into parting with money, to purchase a TILLEY 30 man manual engine. (Tilley of Blackfriars, later to become Shand Mason) a magnificent machine, painted in vermillion and picked out in gold with a sign saying:- Hitchin subscription fire engine 1834. It had 7 inch barrels and a stroke of 8¾ inches. It was capable of delivering approximately 1¼ gallons per stroke.

By 1845 Newton had 3 manuals, the third one being very powerful, having 5 inch barrels and an extremely long stroke. These 3 pumps Newton used at Dead Street (now Queen Street) in 1845. Newton thought he would lose the town to this fire which started at Mr. Langfords ware- house and by its sheer ferocity engulfed a great proportion of the street.

He positioned the 2nd. & 3rd engines on either side of the road at the river in Bridge Street & the Tilley at the river in Dead Str. (now the water board). From there he threw a jet of water that reached the school in Dead Street. He used his No. 1 & 2 engines at fires that are comparable if not bigger than many of todays modern firemen see in their service. One such incident being at Luton Hoo on December 2nd 1843. Newton took 21 of his Brigadiers and 61 volunteers. They pumped for 2 days and consumed 14 gallons of beer and eleven shillings and four pence worth of bread and cheese! His large fire at Dead Str. prompted him to print certain rules for water supplies and access points in the town for the benefit of his Brigadiers.

The "Tilley" 30 man pump.

The occurence which affects all firemen most, is the loss of a colleague, and it would have been the same for Newton and his crew, when Fireman Dawbun was crushed under the wheels of the No: 2 engine, en~route to a farm fire at Weston in 1817. Newton was probably devastated, especially when it came to light that Wm: Moles, 17 years of age was responsible for the act of arson. The judge, Mr. Dallas said he could find no mercy for Moles. He was executed by hanging in the vicinity of his crime. Following this incident Newton got his committee to agree to rules in respect of who should ride the appliances ÷

~ RULES ~

1/ 24 men be appointed to work the engines, and assist in cases of fire.

2/ That such men be renumerated for their services by the fire officer in the usual way.

3/ That on any alarm of fire the men appointed repair to the engine house and such them that shall be named by the churchwardens or agents do ride upon and attend the engines.

4/ That no person other than the men appointed be permitted to ride on any engine.

5/ That the engineer be authorised to require such additional assistance as he may deem necessary.

It is interesting to note that penalties for arson have been stringent from the earliest times. The Romans, when the arsonist was convicted, would clad the offender in TUNICA MOLESTA, a flax garment, covered with pitch or wax which was then ignited! In 1855 a Hertford arsonist received a free ticket to Botany Bay!

When Newtons two manual engines turned out to the great Ashwell fire in 1850, the sight of the engines, pulled by seven horses with postillions, Tom Clark, Jack Webb, Charles Hyde & Jack Hare driving must have been an amazing spectacle. This was the second fire disaster Ashwell suffered. On this occasion flames were reported to cover ½ mile in length and 80 yards deep!

The speed at which fire engines turn out to calls, is a cause of some considerable pride even today. In Newtons day, a certain GEORGE PACK, resident in Sun Street was the "knocker up"; The man who roused the postillions and firemen when the call of fire was given. It is said of George, when made aware of a fire, would light his gas stove and put the kettle on. He would then do his duty, rousing the men. He would then return to his cup of tea before going to the fire where he was responsible for supplying beer to the pump men. A responsible task, considering the possible alternative that without beer the building could be left to burn!

Newtons term of office ended in 1851; 36 years as officer in charge. No officer in charge would exceed that amount of time in office in the future. The only person to appreciate Newtons retirement would be his wife. Who could finally hang out her washing, without fear of it disappearing as the pumps turned out, with Newton crying, "cut the line."

The Solid Silver dish Presented to Isaac Newton Esq.

A s the proverb says,"A new broom sweeps clean". This seems to have been the case after Newton retired in 1851. His position was filled by William Jackson, described as a 'tin' workman living in Bridge street. He probably realised that he would never be totally in command whilst the appliances were situated in Newton's yard. Shortly after taking over, the fire station was moved to the old maltings leading onto the Wratten. There to remain until 1870.

Jackson was to experience the same degree of arson attacks that all firemen suffer, and there is no doubt that "Fire the good friend and bad enemy", formed a fatal fascination for certain people. One such person was a police constable Scott, who was charged with lighting several fires in Hitchin area. He was acquitted, sent to another area, where he was convicted of arson, following a further spate of incendiarism.

In 1853 at Gatwards ironmongers in Market square, the town was to experience one of its earliest recorded deaths by fire. Mr & Mrs. Gatward, awakened from their sleep by fire, began to leave the accomodation above the shop. Mrs Gatward went back to get jewellery, she was overcome and perished. Jackson and his men were soon on the scene with the № 3 engine. A bucket chain was formed from the horse pond in Bridge street along Sun Street and the river by the Biggin. The bucket chain was made up of men passing the full buckets and women and children pass-ing the empty buckets back. It was reported that volunteer pumpers were loath to come forward, following unfounded reports of large amounts of explosives within the shop.

In consequence of material damage having been done to the Engine by overloading it when travelling, you are particularly requested NOT TO ALLOW ANY PERSON to ride on, or lay hold of, the same, except such as are specially appointed.

Hitchin November 16th, 1824.

An early directive from C.F.O Isaac e Newton as to who 'would' ride the pumps. DW

The bucket chain principle was not far from being obsolete. In the Hitchin diary of George Beaver in 1859, a mention is made of a water supply :-"A fire occurs at the White Lion in Sheep market. I turn water on and fire soon subdued and not much damage done, thanks to water works supply". This apparently was the first mention of a water supply in connection with fire.

Although a volunteer Brigade, funds were still needed to supply essential equip--ment. Public subscription was one method, Insurance companies another. Jackson found a novel way of improving his resources. He staged a Fire Brigade show, a satirical light hearted look at the Brigade. Held on the 17th. September 1863 at Hitchin Town hall it was by all accounts a success. Jackson it must be assumed took the leading roll as "Capt. Trougher", James Lewin as the "West End Miller", Fred Mead "The Verdant Butcher" and George Pack as, "The Gallant Tailor". Jackson retired in 1867.

The Fire Brigade show 1863. in aid of funds. Original made of linen and measuring 184mm × 485mm.

Under Distinguished Patronage

THEATRICAL PERFORMANCE
In AID of The Fire Brigade Fund
WILL TAKE PLACE AT
THE TOWN HALL
On Thursday, September 17th 1863.

When James Lewin assumed command of the Brigade in 1867, he was left with a legacy of Newtons equipment, an inventory of which was as follows ÷ Two large engines, a Tilley & Bristow, two small engines (old) prob--ably Newshams,) 800 foot of hose,(which would have been of leather.) One hydrant, one long ladder, eight leather traces, four rope traces, two horse fire buckets, one hand engine, (probably a squirt). 130 leather buckets.

Lewin also moved the location of the fire station in 1870 to the rear of SPURRS shop, in the great yard, now the precinct. The station was desc--ribed as a shed, bare and whitewashed inside, with leather buckets hang--ing on the crossbeams, whilst on the walls were wooden staves that firemen used to carry many years before as well as the bells for the horses and a rusty

The Fire Station
The Great Yard.

cavalry sword rescued from the ashes of the Bendish House fire and a peculiar old shoe from the great fire of Sun Street in 1793.

During this period, Lewin was building a strong relationship with the surrounding Brigades. Having combined drills, and assisting at large fires when they were required. This was a reciprocal arran--gement and by all accounts a cordial affair, As one entry in the Brigade minute book reports, "16th March 1871, at 2:30 p.m. drilled with Baldock volunteer fire Brigade. Brigade in full uniform. Hitchin engine supplied Baldock through 10 lengths easily. Later we dined with Baldock."

The Newton appliances were still in active use at this time, and the insurance companies were still very much of a major factor in the Brigades life. This was shewn in 1867, when the Brigade were called to Mr. Quenby's of Apsley End, Shillington on 25th. February. Seven hay stacks were dest--royed. The stacks were insured by the Royal Farmers insurance who reimbursed the fireman their fees. Taking into account the attendance time of 1 hour, it would seem a very wise decision to have insurance cover! The time was not far off where the villages were to be asked to pay towards the Brigade's upkeep. At this time their contribution to the Brigades services were nothing!

Drills and practices were carried out regularly, and it was not unknown for officers from the London Fire Brigade to attend and watch, advise and "give valuable assistance." One such officer was Fireman. J. A. Ford, another being Supt: Pearce. Supt: Pearce, whose family came from Pirton, had some memorable moments during his service. On one occasion at Hounds--ditch he helped rescue 19 people from a burning building. He was severely injured by falling masonary. Subsequently he was awarded the coveted silver cross by Captain Eyre Massey Shaw.

> ## HITCHIN FIRE ENGINES.
>
> **T**HE HITCHIN LOCAL BOARD HEREBY GIVE NOTICE that it is their intention to make a discretionary CHARGE, pursuant to Sec33 of "The Town Police Clauses Act 1847" for the use OF THE STEAM OR MANUAL FIRE ENGINE, when called to Fires outside their district.
>
> WM. ONSLOW TIMES
> October 23rd, 1889   CLERK TO THE BOARD

Ford was not as fortunate. Having rescued 6 people at a fire in the Grays Inn Road, London on the 7th. October 1871, the escape ladder he was on became enveloped in the flames. He attempted to use the chute at the rear of the ladder, but the hooks on his fire tunic caught in the wire mesh of the chute. He hung there in the flames, finally falling to the ground. He died later from his injuries.

I n 1871 Lewin received a new pump, a 6"inch manual as supplied to the Metropolitan Fire Brigade, (London). As always the men paraded and marched to the station to collect their new Shand & Mason engine. Shand Mason document the engine as, "an early London Brigade pattern, of the size for 22 pumpers. It had single folding levers." Lewin had asked the Lighting inspectors for 2 new engines when they had reported a surplus in their accounts of £70. £50 had been offered for the old engines. Lewin received the one at a cost of £122~4 shillings. It was a powerful engine, which could supply 2 good jets. Records shew it gave, "Great satisfaction" After "washing" the engine, the men were entertained by Mr Wm: Hill jnr: at the Sun Hotel. The Sun Hotel had supplied horses for the fire engines since 1834 and would continue to do so until 23rd March 1917, when the Shilcocks auction would sell the remaining horses belonging to the Sun Hotel. Motor power was taking over.

The Sun Hotel

Times were moving a trifle faster now, new equipment was purchased to improve the Nº 1 engine, which would not lift water, fortunately at a practice drill. The leathers on the buckets were worn and had to be hammered out, and new washers put in the suct-ion, "But the engine did not pump water even then!" It is not the most ideal sight to watch firemen, unable to pump water, as witnessed in 1928 at Pirton, when the Morris~Guy failed. Thankfully this does not happen often.

In 1872 the Brigade was presented with a wheeled escape ladder by The Society of preservation of life from fire, probably a "Wivell" escape.

It was the 18th Century when water mains are mentioned in the London area, probably appearing in Hitchin some time later. Lewin mentions 1868, that at a fire in Queen Street, in out houses belonging to Mrs. Eastwick, the water supply from the fire plug was good enough without using the pump. The fire plug being a literal description of a hydrant.

At this time firemen were only called to fires, very rarely being called upon to undertake other services. They were strictly a fire brigade, whereas today, Fire Brigades undertake numerous other duties and should by rights be called, Fire & Rescue services. Only a few Brigades have adopted this title, and they never dropped the word "Fire" from that title. It is not hard to understand therefore that in Lewins day to attend 10 fires a year was exceptional, but they would all be fires, very rarely rescues. Having claimed that rescues were rarely carried out, it is left to the readers imagin--ation in respect of the following report from a 1927 extract by Barbara Stephen's; "Emily Davies & Girton College", ≈ 1872. When Miss Rachel Susan Cook, afterwards Mrs. C. Scott, formerly of the Ladies College at Benslow, took her tripos in Classics at Cambridge, The students climbed into the roof and rang the alarm bells with such effect that the Hitchin police began to get the firefighters ready for action!!

1871 Shand Mason early London pattern manual engine. Single folding levers, for 22 pumpers.

It would appear that the Metropolitan Brigade influenced Lewin in the wearing of uniform. When he resigned in May 1875, due to his age, His men were equipped with tunics, belts & axes and suction wrenches.

It is nice to note that Mr. Lewin was still active in Brigade circles in 1881, when Captain Chalkley invited him back to inspect the engines.

It must be remembered that when Isaac Chalkley took over the Hitchin Brigade, he did so by way of a vote of confidence from his men. Like a pecking order, men with ability made the natural progression through the ranks, joining as firemen and onward through to the officer ranks. Something which every fire brigade in Britain is justifiably proud of to this day. All chief officers of all brigades started as firemen. So it was that Chalkley took command. He was called, on one hand, a gentleman, and on the other a rigid disciplinarian, mainly due to the "battle lines" he drew up upon taking over. He apparently made it quite clear that he was in charge, spelling out the alternative to non acceptance quite clearly.

In the early days of the Metropolitan Fire Brigade, Firemen worked under the threat of dismissal if they did not attend immediately or threw water over other firemen - plus a fine of 2/6d. Chalkley demanded total loyalty from his fireman, otherwise they would be dismissed! ✂ ✂ ✂ Also at this time the rank of superintendent was replaced by captain. This may have been to distance the volunteer fire brigade from the Paid police force. A point that was forceably stressed by a councillor in 1910. When at the proclamation parade of King George V, the police were not 'invited' to parade, "because we will have to pay them". Alternatively it may have been to follow the line of the London Brigade, who were very much "Navy" orientated.

NOTICE
In case of FIRE the Keys of the ENGINE HOUSE are Kept at Mr I. CHALKLEY BRAND STREET

The fire sign. 15 foot off the ground on the corner of Paynes Park & Old Bank Road

On November 6th 1875, the Brigade were called to Tukes Mill on what is now Windmill Hill. The cause was a small fire in the machinery, usually caused by friction. This occurred at 1:15 p.m. The fire was extinguished, and as is good practice two firemen were left to keep a watch for any further outbreaks. At 4:15 p.m. they pronounced it "all out"! On the 7th November they were recalled to "the mill well alight", which they could do nothing about, as a wind was up, and the mill was too far gone; Timbers and stones crashing through the structure. In 1887 Charlton Mill was destroyed by fire as was Grove Mill in 1889. At the Charlton Mill fire it was reported of the fire, that anything that wasn't made of iron was destroyed, the weight of the corn on the top floor contributed to the collapse of the structure. A large part of the house, belonging to Mr & Mrs. Lewin jnr; was saved.

The mills collapse must have reminded Chalkley of a brush with death he had had sometime earlier in his occupation as an engineer. He achieved nationwide recognition for having successfully moved a windmill to higher ground, having first loaded it on a conveyance. On the second occasion that he attempted this feat, the 23 horses were connected up and the mill was loaded. As a final check Chalkley crawled under the wagon. *Grove Mill* Whilst underneath one of the wheels sunk into the ground, causing the wagon to overturn and in its turn collapsing and smashing the windmill! Chalkley did not move anymore mills, as he had to make good the damage incurred at this incident.

Fires still occur at Mills mainly due to electrical faults although there is the additional risk now days of chemicals being involved such as Chlorine. Following the closure of Bowmans Mill in Walsworth Road in 1982 this left only one working mill in the area, Bowmans Mill, Ickleford.

here is no doubt that putting a uniform on a man tends to reinforce discipline. This is exactly what Chalkley did. His men began to look like firemen, in their brass helmets, long tunics and leather belts & axes. The visits to surrounding brigades continued, as did the drills in the local area, with the escape ladder in the town and the pumps at such sites as Purwell mill.

As his equipment was improving so were his standards. Recruit drills became part of the training before riding the engine. A new hose cart was purchased, which was a single horse carraige with hose carried beneath it. Most of the hose was made of leather and rivetted, but the more flexible canvas hose was starting to make inroads

The hose cart

Although arson has many forms and much publicity, public spirited persons were still in evidence. A certain Mr. Paternoster & Mr Moules successfully extinguished a fire at the Sun Hotel in 1885 before the arrival of the Brigade. No. 2 engine attended, and it was decided to leave 2 firemen on duty "all night", E. Logsdon & C.L. Barham were the "unfortunate" pair detailed. Logsdon and his family had close ties in the catering and management of the Sun Hotel.

Chalkley is credited with the acquisition of the towns first steam appliance, and credit rightly so as the Chief Officer. But behind this achievement was the very forceful character of Edwin Logsdon, the 2nd officer. By drumming up public subscriptions he raised £404 of the £477 require. The remaining money was put up by the water board. On the understanding that the steamer could be used as an alternative to the water boards own pumps. Which by all accounts left a lot to be desired. On April 21st 1887, the men collected their new steamer from the railway station where it had arrived by express train due to the "kindness of Mr. Watkins of the Great Northern Railway". The driver of the steamer was Mr. Hedgeman the representative of the SHAND & MASON C^o. Under his management the engine, christened ST. GEORGE was driven to the Sun Hotel accompanied by the Baldock & Shefford brigades. There to be photographed by the towns leading photographer, T.B. Latchmore

From there the procession proceeded to the Priory Park by the kind permission of Mr. F. Delmé Radcliffe, where its power was shewn to the towns people. The result was impressive. It is reported that 100 pounds pressure was raised in 8 minutes 55 seconds this enabled the engine to throw a jet of water 100 feet high using a 1" inch nozzle also 4 jets using 5/8" nozzles "An inquisitive dog, which getting in the lines of one of the streams was lifted from the ground and turned head over heels several times". This engine

The "St. George" Steamer

was originally destined for the town of Bedford, until the Duke of Bedford presented that town with a "handsome engine with much brass work". It transpired that the engine was extremely difficult to handle due to the 8" inch diameter suction, which tended to "suck up the bottom of the pond rather than the water". St. George had smaller suction and proved itself worthy on many occasions.

On June 23rd. 1887 Chalkley had his proudest moment, when his men and their steamer paraded in QueenVictorias Jubilee celebration at Windsor. The steamer had been sent to Windsor the day before and the horses were to be hired locally. Which caused some problems, the first being when the regular driver allowed an inexperienced fireman to handle the horses. The horses could apparently tell the unfamiliar handler and nearly backed Hitchins steamer through a plate glass window. The second incident happened when Fireman Harry Waller loaded the horses they had loaned, onto the Hitchin train! The owner did not take kindly to his horses being "rustled".

Chalkley got his memorial medal and he was further to parade in the Lord Mayors show in London in 1890, where the Londoners as well as aiming a verbal barrage at the "country boys" did in fact mistake Chalkley, with his full white beard for Captain Eyre Massey Shaw, Chief officer of the London Fire Brigade.

Captain I Chalkley c 1893

The steamer must have seemed God sent to the firemen, they no longer had to stand for hours pumping, as they would of had to at Grove Mill in 1889, where the steamer pumped for 6 hours. It did not save the mill, it was completely burnt out. The mill was a substantial building of four floors, 60 foot long & 25 foot in width. Woodwork on the top floor became ignited when friction from a loose wheel reached a temperature to ignite surrounding woodwork. The Brigade were in attendance within ½ hour of Mr Kendall, the miller, having sent a messenger to alert the Brigade. Having raised steam en- route, water was applied within 2 minutes of arrival. Much of the adjoining mill house was saved, mainly it was claimed because of the presence of such an engine." The mill was insured for £2000 by the Sun Fire Office, whose local agent was Mr. James Shilcock. The use of the steamer caused the occurence of barn & stack fires to go down considerably as the "BEER" pumpers were no longer req- -uired. It became very evident to all concerned that the majority of the previous farm fires were 'set' by the aforementioned for free beer.

On the day of writing this the 22nd. of January 1988, the town had its first unexpected snowfall of the year and the modern appliance was ordered to a road traffic accident on the A505 road at Offley. There to become stranded on the icy hill, fortun- ately successfully having released a driver trapped in his lorry by his legs following a collision with a bus. An interesting analogy occured on December 30th. 1886. Where the Brigade were called to three fires simultaneously at Langley and Langley Bottom. The snow was a foot deep and the Brigade "walked the greater part of the way". Fireman Bennett "Ran over to Langley from Hitchin", having missed the engine!

Escape extending ladder, with wire mesh chute 1872.

In 1891 Chalkley attended one of his largest fires, which occurred at Fosters Yard Bancroft , and which enveloped Elliss & Everards stables and lofts. 3 jets of water were got to work from hydrant & the river at the rear of Russells tanyard. 5 horses were saved, as were some pigs.

On March 20th. 1895, Capt. Chalkley resigned, due to his advancing years. He had attended 85 fires in his 29 years of service. He lived to a ripe old age of 88, and at his funeral in 1913, the Brigade paraded in full uniform.

On February 22nd 1912 a contingent of Fire Brigades paraded outside a house called Sunningdale in the Bedford Road. The Brigades present included, Stevenage, Shefford, Baldock, Buntingford & Royston. They were there to pay their last respects to the Hitchin Fire Brigade Chief Officer, Capt: EDWIN LOGSDON. Who having served 52 years with the brigade, from the age of 17, had recently died. Affectionately named by his second officer as, "Fire & Water", he had died, "in harness", having taken part in drills only six days previously. They gave him a firemans funeral, the oak coffin being transported on the manual pump with his silver helmet on top; Followed by the brigades mentioned above led by Supt: Haddow of the Shefford Brigade.

Logsdon, during his 17 years as Chief officer achieved much; Every man deserves an epitaph, Logsdons stands in Paynes Park.—

Hitchin Fire Station Paynes Park 1904

The old Fire Station; for which he was entirely responsible, albeit with generous support of the towns people and council subscriptions. There were 105 donations, totalling over £600 of the £711 required. The council gave £211 as well as the site. Such personages of the time as Mr. Fenwick Harrison of Kings Waldenbury donated £100. Trinity College, Cambridge £50. Mr. J. Reynolds, Dep.Chief Constable £—10s-6& Frank Carling the proprietor of the town newspaper 2 guineas. With these and many other donations he was able to lay the foundation stone in Paynes Park in 1903 and to see the station completed in 1904, in time to commemorate the coronation of Edward VII. Built it must be stated by Fosters the builders of Hitchin.

Mr. Blood the architect of the new station described it as, "having a frontage of 70 feet, a fitted lavatory, a copper and coal bunker, a hose cleansing room, and a drill yard with a hydrant. 4 rooms over the station including the capts; office, work shops, store and another room for firemens meetings". The appliance room had patent glazed tiles, some brown, some white and a wood block floor.

This station and further innovations were directly due to Logsdon. He made it his business to visit provincial stations to gather ideas on pumps & stations and even to spend weekends at Holborn Fire station, in London and riding their pumps at the invitation of Supt: Pearce; M.F.B.

Euphoria reigned that night of celebration at Paynes Park on the 24th. December 1904. Wine appears to have flowed freely. Councillor Moules, "was so proud" he said, "the Fire Brigade could have anything they wanted!— but he was against un-necessary expenditure!" His ghost must still haunt the council chambers today!

Hitchin Fire Brigade

GRAND OPENING
OF
The New Fire Station,
BY
HER GRACE THE DUCHESS OF BEDFORDE, K.D
WHO WILL BE ACCOMPANIED BY
THE CROWN PRINCE WILHELM (of romantic disposition),
THE GRAND DUKE BERNHARDT; HSH PRINCESS EDERMEA
and the Nobility of the Neighbourhood
ON JUNE 31ST 1904.

The "spoof" programme for the opening of the new fire station (Front cover)

However all was not 'rosy'. Logsdon was continually in contention with council policy, especially with the Reverend Gainsford. On one occasion having to remind councillors that his men were all volunteers and in some cases as Hitchin businessmen they held better positions than the councillors themselves. In some cases he was a trifle too forthright. He once stated that fire engines "were better in use", which incensed a reader of the local paper when this was printed. A letter was written claiming that Logsdon was encouraging arsonists. He was very upset by this and personally went to Bedford, from where the letter originated to speak with the writer! He never found him!!

O ne particularly acrimonious event which caused some concern between the council and the fire brigade was when Logsdon tendered his resig- -nation following criticism of attendance times to a fire at Ransoms stables, Nightingale Road in 1905. The time taken to attend was 30 mins. Councillor Gainsford demanded to know why it had taken 30 minutes to attend Nightingale Road, when at a previous fire at Stotfold it had only taken 13 minutes to attend. To add insult to injury Gainsford claimed the outbreak of fire at Nightingale Road, could of been adequately dealt with by one man with a standpipe and a length of hose!

Logsdon claimed in response that there was difficulty getting horses. When looking deeper into this incident, certain facts come to light that shew Logsdon was trying to change the Brigades establishment. At the time in question Logsdon and Barham, his second officer were actually on the station when the alarm was given. He had also written the following letter to the council two years earlier in 1903.

Curricle Escape Ladder

"As the town grows towards Ickleford and Walsworth, & the Avenue with persons of importance. Consideration to them as the largest rate payers is surely due. A resi- -dent fireman would go to the fire with the hose reel or fire escape, which carries a standpipe and hose with- -out waiting for the rest of the firemen. Others are disadvantaged by running to the station in heavy uniforms. THE HIGHEST IMPORTANCE IS TO TACKLE THE FIRE IN ITS INFANCY." (authors capitals.)

He went on to quote the rateable values of surrounding parishes com- -paring them to similar parishes in surrounding counties, the majority of whom paid for their Fire Brigades upkeep.

The council 'persuaded' Logsdon to withdraw his resignation. Within one year Fm Jacob Reynolds was appointed resident fireman at a rent of £8 per year. As for a horse being stabled at the fire station, this the council considered was "out of the question, as it may not be used for another 3 months!

During his tenure Logsdon was responsible for increasing the amount of equipment including new uniform plus overcoats and caps. A curricle escape ladder, a new jump sheet (£4~2~6d) from Merryweathers and enough hose to stretch from the horse pond in Bridge Street for 725 yards. The installation of more alarm posts in the town, connected to the fire station and alarm bells in the firemens houses. He continued the traditional November 5th annual general meeting, which had been started by his predecessor Chalkley to commemorate the churchwardens "watching for fires" on that date years before. When the towns people celebrated the disc- -overy of the gunpowder plot in 1605. It had been held up to this time at The Angels vaults in Sun Street. Now that Logsdon had his new fire station it was held there. Primarily to inform members of the Brigades business, it was also the major social function of the year for the volunteers. There they would eat pork pies & savoury bread along with the infamous onions. A reminder of a fire they attended in 1881 at St Ippolytts, Where drunken villagers pelted them with onions. One of several incidents that happened at St. Ippolytts over the years! As is a firemans 'lot' to this day, there were many occasions when their meal was interrupted and left uneaten. by the call of FIRE !

1903 Parish	Year	Population	Rateable Value
Pirton	1901	1016	£3: 420
Ickleford	1891	529	2: 187
St Ippolytts	1901	894	5: 911
Holwell	1901	278	2: 972
Gt. Wymondley	1901	279	5: 131
Lt. Wymondley	1891	411	4: 102
Willian	1891	254	2: 577
Letchworth	1891	79	1: 282
Preston	1891	230	1: 363
Kings Walden	1891	1124	5: 506
Langley	1891	152	1: 008
Offley	1891	1268	6: 266
Hexton	1891	167	1: 319
Walsworth	?	?	3: 943
		Total	£47: 067

Rateable Value Urban district £48: 304.

Alarm Post

Logsdon attended many incidents, several of which were unusual as
well as serious in their nature. Shortly after taking over from
Chalkley, the Brigade was called out on 30th May 1895 to a thatched
roof alight at Burgess End Pirton, which had been struck by
lightning during a storm. Because of the lack of telegraphic comm-
-unication between Pirton and Hitchin, a messenger was sent, one
John Thrussell from Pirton. Within 8 minutes of the call being
received the Brigade was on the way. In the meantime the fire had
spread to the adjoining cottages and it was obvious they could not
be saved. Mr Pearce, lost all of his furniture, and George Roberts
and his brother, both deaf and dumb suffered the same misfortune.
Furniture was salvaged from the 3rd cottage
belonging to Thomas Banes. The rain was torrential,
and the water so deep at one point on the Hitchin
to Pirton Road that it extinguished the fire under
the boiler of the steam fire engine!
One thousand feet of hose was used from the
pond. Nearby six labourers working in the fields took
refuge beside a wheat rick which was subsequently
struck by lightning; it killed George Downham instantly and burned
John Weedon so severely that it was doubtful if he would survive.

In February 1898 a call was received from the Sun Hotel, Logsdons
own premises, where fire had broken out in the loft of the old post stables.
The risk of the fire spreading was very high and even today the Hotel
is classed as a high risk.

Adjoining the Sun Hotel was the Angel, then the property of Mr.
Moules, one of the oldest buildings in the town, and storing at that
time, wood and faggots and, abutting these premises was the warehouse
of Henry Barham where Gunpowder & cartridges were stored
Fortunately the premises were saved, but Logsdons stable roof was
burned right off. The cost of the damage was £150. Later at 3-30 in the
morning a further call to a fire was made, in close vicinity to the
first call. This time the carriage works of Mr.
Walter Odell were ablaze. The firemen who had
been standing by at the Sun Hotel, hurried to the
fire with their manual engine, whilst the other
firemen were being called. £260 damage was
caused. Then in 1899 a disastrous fire occurred
at Mr. Quenby's in Bucklesbury, caused by a
boy who was sent to fetch paraffin. He dropped
the candle he was carrying to light his way and the building burst into
flames. The spread of fire was rapid throughout the surrounding ware-
-houses of Nichols the fruiterers, Sharp the pork butcher & the Singer
sewing machine Co.. They were soon destroyed by the fire.

Efforts were made to stop the spread of fire in Tilehouse street
where it had reached the cart shed of Mr. Taylor the Baker. Fm. Barham
had a narrow escape, when the roof on which he was standing collapsed,
"precipitating" him into the fire. His outstretched arms caught on the
rafters of the floor below and saved him! £1000 worth of damage
was incurred at this fire, which reportedly caused GREAT PANIC.

When Logsdon died in 1912 the council asked Charles Loftus Barham the lieutenant to take his place as the Captain. He had several attributes 🏅. He was a first class engineer having served in the Merchant navy aboard the S.S. Faraday as marine engineer. He was an expert on boilers and was totally dedicated to the Brigade. It was not unknown for him to repair the steamer of the neighbouring Brigade, Shefford.

It was Barham who would see the Brigade through the Great War of 1914~18 and to lose three of his colleagues to that tragic event.

Emergency plans for the war effort were slow to come to fruitition in 1914, and until the enemy zeppelins made their assault on England it appears that it was not wholly realised that the war was also upon the civilian pop-

C.L. BARHAM, Engineer, Hitchin

All kinds of
Machinery Repaired
Engines Re-tubed
Fireboxes Fixed
&c.

AGENT FOR ALL THE PRINCIPAL MAKERS

The Barham Family Logo.

-ulation. Zeppelins were witnessed over Hitchin on the 3rd September 1915 & 31st January 1916, and bombs were dropped in Walsworth and Bedford Road during a later raid in 1917. The zeppelins roamed with impunity over the countryside, and although today they appear antiquated, at the time they were the latest "killing" machine, technology of the time had produced. The Brigade were called to stand by during these raids, sometimes for the greater part of the night. Positive arrangements were made to call in a back up crew if the Brigade were out. Documents shew that Mr Watson, the tobacconist, Mr. F. Webb, the chemist (Sun Str:) Mr Crees, the fishmonger or Mr. Clouting, were to be called when the Brigade were absent. Following the successful "downing" of a zeppelin by by Lt: Wm: Leefe Robinson, R.F.C, for which he was awarded the Victoria Cross, The Brigade were instructed by the war office to salvage as much as possible of the structure of any crashed zeppelin. The amount of wood in the structure indicated that Germany was short of aluminium. A sure sign that their war effort was under pressure.

Here at Hitchin, Councillor Frank Newton (twice removed from Isaac Newton, the first chief officer) was querying the Brigades efficiency, asking "if any firemen were capable of carrying down people from high buildings?" and that it took 3 months in London to train men to be able to carry people down a ladder. The metropolitan brigade always chose sailors as firemen because of their ladder experience." He also asked if any of the men were qualified in first aid and if any consideration had been given to connecting telephones in the firemens houses?

As has been well documented, the population as a whole thought the war in the beginning was a great adventure. The Brigade personnel were no exception, taking part in recruiting drives along with other organisations such as the police and St. Johns ambulance Brigade. 15 Firemen were to enlist during the war period. 3 of them never to return.

Carry down

ireman Seymour joined the R.A.S.C, fireman Garrett the Middlesex Hussars. Fireman Jacob Reynolds enlisted under the "Lord Derby scheme". Fm. Langford joined the 1st. Herts; regiment and was seen off to the railway station by his colleagues on the steamer. On the 3rd August 1916 he was killed in action, having reached the rank of C°Sgt. Major, he was buried at Festubert. Fm. Maurice Barker, too young to bear arms for his country, joined the Friends Ambulance and died of "blood poisoning" at Dunkirk. Fm Garrett also gave his life in action.

Criticisms were being made in regard to obtaining horses. The council observed that "several years ago the three major hotels in the town could supply 45 horses, now if 7 were available it would be fortunate." An agreement was reached with the Royal Engineers signal unit at Bearton camp to supply mules for the duration of the war. Colonel Rose, the O/c of the camp stressed that their mules were for "driving & riding" and not for "long reins". Consequently many practices were made with the mules in harness to the steamer. The steamer which weighed 2 tons, was supposed to be pulled by 4 horses, which prompted strong comments by a counc- illor when observed to be, "having a rare old job to get up Hitchin Hill". pulled by only 2 horses! (At the recent celebration of the St George steamer in 1987. The Shand Mason steamer, pulled by two horses was in difficulty pulling up the Priory-by-pass. The steamer crew had to dismount and be picked up by the modern appliances.)

Hitchin War Memorial 1922

On November 20th 1919 Ickleford Manor burnt down whilst being reno- vated by Messrs: Waring & Gillow. The steamer pumped "tons of water" during the 6 hours it was at the fire. Masonary was falling around the firemen as they fought the blaze. Several firemen it is reported fell into deep sewage trenches nearby. The fire it was later ascertained started in a chimney in the plumbers room. Mr Doughty the owner, was in 1922 still proceeding with court action against Waring & Gillow for damages in excess of £30000.

Firemen by their very nature will find the funny side of most incidents they attend. One such occurrence was to a fire at Powells & Son in Bucklesbury (the son was later to become the Chief Officer of the brigade) on the 24th April 1915. It was reported that a person was trapped on the window ledge of the first floor of the premises. Did the Brigade rescue the person? NO. Soldiers from Bearton camp, formed a PYRAMID and carried out the rescue! Some of the soldiers had been firemen in their own home towns before enlisting in the forces. One in particular, Quartermaster Sergeant McDonald pulled the hose cart from the horse pond in Bridge Street to Bucklesbury. French's timber yard was struck by lightning in 1915, once again the mains water supply was insufficient and the river had to be dammed at the rear of "Elses" Laundry. The steamer pumped for 8 hours. The lack of pressure in the towns water mains on several occasions caused great concern with the Fire Brigade & the council. Mr Davey the water engineer had given assurances in the past in respect of pressure and supply in the water mains. Having failed to fulfil his guarantees at a previous fire in Hollow Lane, a councillor accused the water engineers' guarantees as, "All wind and Humbug". Davey was to go on to be another Chief Officer.

POWELL SON

The chronic shortage of horses during the war led the Brigade to accept the offer of a Mercedes car in 1916 as the tractor unit for the steamer and escape ladder. It required considerable modification to bring it up too an acceptable standard, and modifications were carried out by Firemen Cain & Davey at a cost of £225. The motor was a 45 h.p. and was quite the envy of other brigades. The Chief Constable of Walsall enquiring about its suitability in 1920. Davey insisted that it kept its solid tyres stating that, "he would not even go on a joy ride in it if it had pneumatic tyres."

In 1918 the 'coffee pot' steamer, St.George so called by Stevenage people when it was purchased in 1887, failed to pass its boiler inspection. This nec--essitated a replacement. The Brigade would

The Mercedes towing the steamer. an extending ladder was a later fitment. The bell was a gift from F. Newton in memory of his grandfather. The lamps were from Second officer Chalkley. The scond lamps from J. Blood. Speedometer from James Knight

have dearly loved to be motorised as were their colleagues at Letchworth, with their Dennis fire engine, acquired in 1914, before the war caused a shortage of materials. Therefore Hitchin had to accept the Shand & Mason offer of an improved design steamer at a cost of £530. It could raise a jet 150 feet and do the equivalent work of 4, 20 man manual engines. The old engine was exchanged for £60 and had given 31 years service. The new steamer was to serve until 1929, when it was made redundant and reportedly sold to Fireman H. Barham for £10.

In 1912 at Walsworth the firemen shewed their generosity when they paid the fees incurred at the fire from their own pockets, when it was found that the owner was uninsured. For the same incident the Sun Hotel only charged half the normal fee for the use of their horses.

1914 saw W.H.Spencers Iron Foundry in Walsworth road, well alight causing £800 damage and the use of 600 foot of hose from the hydrant at Bowmans Mill. On the 3rd March 1915 a tremendous explosion was heard from Newtons shop when a burning-off lamp was knocked over.

The Barham and Newton business establishments were in close proximity in Tilehouse street. Whether there was any personal animosity between them will probably never be known but the newspapers of the time were regularly printing letters of criticism concerning the running of the Brigade, the charging for services & mismanage--ment of monies. These criticisms originated from Mr. F. Newton, grandson of Isaac, and it would appear were directed at C.L.Barham junior, the Brigade secretary. Barham stated,

1912 Letchworth

"Why Mr. Newton should so constantly seek a pretext to attack the Fire Brigade passes my comprehension. He has had good reason to be thankful for their services. In 1913 the firemen were called to Mr. Newton's property upon no fewer than three occasions. In no case did the firemen receive any payment for their services. On the contrary, they paid for the privelege of saving a large and valuable haystack, which was not insured. Having incurred a liability of £1-5s in respect of horse hire and other expenses, the Brigade, who had worked hard during the night for six hours, naturally expected Mr. Newton to pay. He declined to do so. In the end the firemen themselves paid out of their own pockets, thus preventing the amount being charged to the rates." *Express Newspaper, December 1921*

On the lighter side the Barham family definitely had their moments during their fire fighting careers. On the 29th May 1921 a call to the Herbert Frost antique gallery in Sun Street, found C.L.Barham junior hurrying through the gallery with Frosts dog firmly affixed to the seat of Barham jnr:s' pants. In 1899 when Barham jnr; was the call boy for Logsdon he was reported for actually "holding up" the Royal Mail Coach when it was about to run over the hose lines at a fire at Fishers' Sweet Factory in Walsworth Road.

On one occasion at the town hall C.L.Barham jnr; was punched in the eye by one Charles Spicer for no apparent reason. His father and an off duty policeman came to his aid and escorted the offender away. But not before he had attempted to," gnaw Barham jnr:s finger to the bone"

The town hall had been the source of aggravation to the firemen on several occasions. Besides the previously mentioned occurrence they were also stopped from inspecting the fire extinguishers by the Rev: Gainsford and ordered off the stage.

They were also seen at one event refusing to let the elder citizens access to a performance, claiming that the town hall was full up. One irate member of the public wrote to the press saying, that after being refused entry he had seen the Firemen allowing Young Ladies access to the performance!

The Town Hall.

On the 31st July 1921 at 68 years of age C.L.Barham senior, Chief fire officer died. He was brought back from St:Bartholomews hospital London on the Mercedes accompanied by the 3rd: officer, A. Foster, Fireman Seymour, Fm. J. Waldock & Fm. J. Reynolds. Only a fortnight earlier whilst discussing his 50 years service he had said," he wanted to die a Fireman". His wish was granted.

At his funeral at St Marys Church, Hitchin, the older part of the town was closed and contingents of the Shefford, Baldock, Stevenage & Letchworth Brigades attended, led by their respect- -ive chief officers. His devotion to duty was shewn by the fact that up until July 29th, the day he was taken into hospital, he had not slept away from home since 1887, When he had accompanied the steamer to Windsor. For 34 Years he had stated that he did not wish to be away from the town when a FIRE occurred. He could not be persuaded even to take a weekend away because of this dedication to the Hitchin Fire Brigade.

Barhams
"Last Call"

When Barham died in 1921, J.T. Chalkley was asked to stand as Chief Fire officer. He did so on the understanding that it would be for a short term only, due to his age. He resigned in fact shortly after taking office for that very reason. The 2nd officer, A. Foster was requested to stand as C.F.O. in Chalkleys place, which he did.

Foster remarked when he took office that the Brigade was being mis-managed, and it was his intention to correct this state of affairs.

Since the demise of C.F.O. Barham, criticism had been aimed at C.L. Barham junior, the brigade secretary. With his father dead, the 'knives' were out in earnest. This along with the acrimonious exchanges with F. Newton led to his resignation. It is hard to believe that a man who had served the Brigade man and boy, who was a prolific writer of Fire Brigade history for the local press and it must be assumed gave Mr Reginald Hine historical details of the Brigade, could be treated this way. Never the less with the threat of solicitors action if Brigade documents were not returned, the Barham connection with the Brigade was all but over. Only one brother remained in the Brigade and he would leave shortly afterwards. In C.L. Barhams place

Captain A. Foster

as secretary stood W.G. Grant, who was to hold this post until the second world war when the voluntary brigades were disbanded.

Within one year of taking office Foster was to resign in November 1922, after 41 years service. He had taken the advice of an 'eminent oculist' who had told him that the "excitement would have very serious results". Two years later ex-C.F.O. Foster was tragically killed instantly beneath the wheels of a brewery lorry in Bridge Street.

Taking Fosters place was Mr. John Davey, who in his civilian occupation was the towns water engineer, which was an asset in his selection. His rise to C.F.O. had been rapid, as he had only started with the Brigade in 1910. He had also been in trouble with the Urban District Council. In 1904, he had claimed that he could "up" the pressure in the water mains by 40 lbs. on request. Something he failed to do in February 1906, when the Brigade requested increased pressure at a fire at Shambrooks, Hitchin Hill. As a result two cottages were lost. A quote from the Brigade minute book says, "Davey was much to blame for not pumping water following a request from the fireground. The council had him on the carpet to explain matters. I am told he had a rough time of it."

The Morris Guy, reg no: NK 7620.

Davey is reported to have been a popular officer, but it is doubtful he was as popular with the council when in 1923 he threatened to resign if the council did not consider purchasing a Motor Fire engine, especially considering the state of the present appliances. It was considered, and subsequently the MORRIS GUY was purchased. Davey stressed that no responsible fire brigade had pumps of less than 250 gallons per minute capacity. The Morris Guy had only 150-250. g.p.m.

19

JOHN DAVY

Davey wanted a Merryweather with a much larger capacity pump. Merryweather were an established quality fire engine company, and this was reflected in the price of £1500. Whereas the Morris Guy was priced at £800. When the Morris Guy was displayed in Hitchin even the towns people disapproved of it. When tested against the steamer, it was reported that it, "performed as well as intended by the manufacturers". On the other hand the steamer was, "an unqualified success". The council were not to be moved on their decision, which brought caustic comments against them in later years, accusing them, "of amateur interference in the choice of the engine". Mr Harry Cannon wagered £50 that any two councillors could operated the pump.

Merryweather and

Davey had to live with his doubt about the Morris Guy, although it performed well in 1925 at Russells tanyard in Bancroft where along with the Letch-worth motor and the Stevenage steamer a large fire was successfully "brought under".

One of Daveys biggest fires which he attended was out of the Hitchin area at Messrs. Maythorns Motor Works, Biggleswade, where Hitchin set into open water ¼ of a mile from the fire. £100,000 of damage was incurred. Also attending the fire was Luton, Bedford, Sandy, Potton, Henlow aerodrome & the Biggleswade Brigades

Davey left the Brigade in 1926 due to conflicting interests with his regular employment at the waterworks. He was 52 years of age. On the 17th December 1933, Davey died. J. T. Chalkley the caretaker Chief officer died 3 months later on the 17th March 1934, he had been 66 years of age when he had assumed command following Barhams death.

Jacob Reynolds now occupied the C.F.O position, having been Daveys 2nd officer. He was to hold this position for two years until his resignation in 1928. During this period he achieved the appointment of a residential fireman on the station at Paynes Park. Fm Fisher & his wife were to feature eminently in the running of the fire station and social club, which was instigated on the 20th January 1927. Mrs Fisher provided refreshments every Thursday evening when the club opened.

The club consisted of 6 honorary members, 2 off-icers & 12 firemen. The social facilities have continued over the years at Hitchin Fire Station from that day forward. Fm Fishers duties were:

1/ TO BE EMPLOYED BY THE WATERWORKS.
2/ TO CLEAN THE CATTLE PENS ON A WEDNESDAY
3/ TO DEVOTE THE REST OF HIS TIME TO CLEANING THE FIRE ENGINES AND EQUIPMENT.

The Herts & Beds Bacon Factory Nightingale Road,

In 1926 the Herts & Beds Bacon factory in Nightingale Road had its roof damaged by fire. The Morris Guy and steamer worked well. Fireman Garrett lacerated two fingers but persevered in his duties.

20

On May 22nd 1927 an incident occurred at the old Vicarage in the churchyard involving chemicals. Possibly the first that the Brigade had to contend with. Water had entered builders lime, causing it to slake and ignite nearby logs. After extinguishing the fire the report was written as follows: "After thorough inspection of the building which is the property of Mr. Harry Cannon. The Brigade returned to the station at 8-40 p.m. Where the lime that had settled in their throats was removed (TO THEIR SATISFACTION)"

An awareness was growing of fires involving petroleum spirits. Mr. Kemp was appointed as the petroleum officer by the council. Conflicts between the Brigade and Council still arose, C.F.O. Reynolds wanted the rear of the station extended to obtain more room to house the escape ladder and to allow his men to 'rig' in safety. It was reported that the firemens boots were often run over by the appliance due to the present arrangement. He wanted full uniform supplied and some extra hose. Most of which he received. He tried the councils patience by pur--chasing a Davy escape line ~ without the councils permission and was reprimanded. This was indicative of the councils desire to be "master" of the VOLUNTEERS This escape line along with an extension ladder that the firemen purchased themselves, was a means of shewing their defiance.

Spring snap hook
Braking Mechanism
Cotton covered steel cable
Cable reel
steel slide
A Davy Escape line

1927 saw Highdown House, Pirton, severely damaged by fire, although a good quantity of books and furniture was salvaged. At a fire at Langley Bottom in the same year the hose froze solid and the pond was pumped dry in an effort to extinguish 3 hay stacks. On the 15th April 1927, a man was arrested at the Holwell turning, accused of Arson. The evidence against him ~ he was "armed with a piece of IRON and a lump of COAL". When arrested he escaped from the side car of the police motor cycle, only to be recaptured later.

In 1928 C.F.O. Reynolds accused his 2nd officer Green, of discussing committee business in public. Green subsequently resigned. The whole matter was investigated by the Brigade secre--tary, W.G. Grant. C.F.O. Reynold was "invited" to explain the circumstances to the council. The outcome of which was his own resignation. It would appear that Reynolds was vindicated in the end when in the 1930s he was made Hon. Chief Officer as the last surviving C.F.O; and appointed as a judge of the competition drills that the Brigade took part in.

The Holwell Arsonist

Once again the Brigade was leaderless; Since Barham had died there had been a succession of short term officers.

The council were looking for a steadying influence to run the Brigade and they found it in Fireman Don Powell. Elected by his companions in the fire brigade, this nomination had still to be ratified. Powell had conditions of his own before he would accept this position. The prime one being the appointment of an engineer to maintain the appliances. This position was filled by Fm Reed. Mrs. Fisher continued to be "mother" to the firemen, mending tunics and sewing buttons on.

21

Powell accepted the rank of Captain in June 1928. He was to remain there until 1939. He of all the chief officers would see most changes in the Brigade. Some of the largest fires and the complete mechanisation of the Brigade. Powell had the added problem of re-instilling the spirit of the men following the Reynolds-Green affair.

The Morris Guy was still a 'thorn in the side' with the firemen. It performed satisfactory in the town at fires such as the one that occurred at 1:15 a.m, August 21st. 1928. A Terrific blaze was reported at Sharps photo studio, in the High Street. Mr.&Mrs. Sharp had reason to be thankful to their cat which alerted them to the blaze. Hitchin with the Morris Guy & steamer were assisted by Stevenage and Letchworth Brigades. It was soon "brought under", but not before considerable damage had been caused by fire spread, to the Singer Machine company, David Greigs & the Pearl Assurance offices.

C.F.O Jacob Reynolds 1928

On the 5th. October 1928 both the Morris and the steamer were called to the Shoulder of Mutton public house, Pirton ~ thatch alight. The Morris Guy was "in attendance" in approximately 7 minutes. The firemen set their suction into the pond ¼ mile distant. Two firemen were on the thatch with their hose, but the pump would not lift water! The steamer arrived and was set to work, but it was too late. The public house dating back to 1510 was destroyed, as was the Brigades reputation and their confidence in their appliances.

A great deal of criticism has been aimed at the Morris Guy, in as much as it wasn't commended in the first place by C.F.O.Davey. As Mr.Harry Cannon stated to the council, the pump was "originally purchased for the town only". It must be remembered that this motorised engine was the "beginning of the end" of the steam engines, and the firemen were not overly impressed. The unfortunate thing appears to be that nobody was fully conversant with the complexities of this new turbine pump. And it would appear, there was a total ignorance in respect of the valves in the reciprocating primer. Which were found to be jammed with dirt when the manufact--urers representative inspected them.

On 17th May 1929, C.F.O. Powell arranged a test drill with the Morris Guy to attempt to salvage some of the Brigades pride, following the Pirton fire. He arranged with a Mr.Franklin who owned a condemned cottage at Pirton to delib--erately ignite it, and for the Morris Guy to attempt

Leyland F.E.1. Reg.No. UR 5718

to put it out. Before the engine left the station, C.F.O Powell & Mr.Prime gave it a thorough check and inspection. It arrived at Pirton 9 minutes after leaving Hitchin. At the first attempt the pump would not lift water. When moved to another pond it lifted muddy water with no trouble. This did not placate the Firemen, who handed the council a vote of no confidence in the Morris Guy. C.F.O. Powell never trusted the engine from then on. An academic move as in 1929 the Leyland F.E.1. arrived.

aving surpassed two other appliances during testing, a Dennis and Simonis, the Leyland was accepted as a replacement for the steamer. The acceptance tests involved pulling a 25 cwt. trailer up Offley Hill and then towing it down the hill to test the brakes. The Morris Guy was relegated to second pump and left for town duties, the original concept. The Paynes Park Fire Station was now fully motorised. The Leyland as number 1 pump had cost £1191≈2/≈ exclusive of the windscreen. It had a 400 gallon per minute pump, a great improvement on the Morris Guys 250 g.p.m. To accom--odate these appliances the station had to be redesigned. The arched frontage was change to one large opening in 1930.

Nº2 Foam Branch & knapsack tank.

Visitors from the continent were amazed at the amount of work the volunteers undertook, a point Powell and his predecessors had always stressed. The Brigade was getting busier and purchasing new equipment, such as a Pyrene foam generator at £30 & 10 gallons of solution at 27/6d per gallon. Also purchased was the very useful Seibe Gorman salvus breathing sets 3 of which cost £55≈11≈5d This equipment was to be increasingly used in the coming years, and was to replace the patent smoke helmet. A great deal of this equipment was purchased with the advice and assistance of the NATIONAL FIRE BRIGADE ASSOCIATION of which the Brigade were now members, the U.D.C. having paid the subscription fee. The council also came to agreement with the rural districts such as St. Ippolytts & Arlesly to test their hydrants, also for the Brigade to undertake special services, such as floodings and ammonia leaks as occurred at Coopers butchers shop in Tilehouse street.

On October 8th. 1932, a fire at Messrs: Powells, Bucklesbury, damaged the shop to the expense of £1000 and on the 16th. December 1933, Welbury School at Lt: Offley was severely damaged by fire. The gymnasium, Chapel and power house were destroyed. The bell tower was pulled down by the Brigade to stop the spread of fire. A 500 gallon oil tank also blew up. C.F.O. Powell with his mistrust of the Morris Guy and the fact that the town would be left without fire cover sent for the Letchworth Brigade who attended with their Dennis engine & trailer pump. The Brigade spent 11 hours at this fire. On this fire along with a length of hose the Brigade lost its jump sheet On the 24th. January 1934, Fireman Sale

The Jumping Sheet (morywether) 12 men minimum. 30 foot maximum. Hold the sheet by the beckets, arms outstretched, palms down. Feet together lean backwards. Look straight ahead. O/c gives order TAUT SHEET as person jumps. The jumper should look straight ahead and step off with his left foot he should remain in the upright position and land on the balls of his feet. The use of the jumping sheet was abandoned by the N.F.S.

crashed the Mercedes into a brick wall in Nutleigh Grove, whilst going to a fire in the fog. With him were Fm. C. French & Appleby, all received minor injuries. The Mercedes was a "write off". On the 5th March 1934 the Brigade purchased from SALES GARAGE a 21 H.P. Sunbeam car as a replacement at a cost of £40!!

23

Even at this early date the prospect of another war was being considered, only 16 years after the cessation of the last conflict. Home office circ-ulars in respect of preparations for air~raids were requested.

The population in 1934 was 15000, and the rateable value £105000. The area covered was 3675 acres. The damages by fire were ÷

	IN DISTRICT	OUT OF DISTRICT
1932 =	£1258	£2088
1933 ≈	£138	£515

In the same year Jacob Reynolds was made honorary C.F.O; as the only surviving C.F.O. His son Fm.E.Reynolds continued to win the British Legion Challenge SHIELD in competition drills.

Ambulance classes were started and once again war precautions were discussed as indicated in 1936, when 6 Auxilary firemen were needed in case of a national emergency.

In 1935 the cost of running the Hitchin volunteer Fire Brigade was ÷

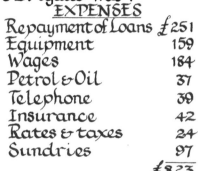

Deibe Gorman
calvus
B.el.set.
1930.

EXPENSES		RECEIPTS	
Repayment of Loans	£251	Towns rates	£771
Equipment	159	Charge for appliances	
Wages	184		£52
Petrol & Oil	37		
Telephone	39		
Insurance	42		
Rates & taxes	24		
Sundries	97		
	£823		£823

The 22 fires attended in 1935 comprised, ÷ 3 cornfields, 2 grass, 2 hay~-stacks, 2 factories, 1 lorry, 1 car, a shop & a market garden storehouse.

From this date on C.F.O: Powells most trying times were to begin. On the 26th. March 1938, the E.S.A, factory caught fire, causing £50,000 damage. The Leyland pump operated for 17 hours! At an incident to E.S.A in 1907 much criticism was aimed at the Stevenage council when it became apparent that Hitchins modern equipment did not fit Stevenages old fashioned hydrants. BRASS HELMETS were on the way out due to the danger of electrical conduction. This may have been due to the experience of Sir Aylmer Firebrace (shortly to become responsible for the National Fire Service) the future C.F.O London Fire Brigade. Who had witnessed a fireman electrocuted because of a brass helmet. The full time volunteers at Hitchin had been increased to 10, and 45 auxilary firemen had been recruited. Their equipment was slowly arriving

1936
AFS
HITCHIN

The Fire Brigade Act 1938 was to change the face of the voluntary Brigades in a big way. The London Fire Brigade officers who were briefed to ascertain the readiness of the rural brigades in the event of war, were reportedly appalled by what they found, even the larger brigades were found to be lacking in leadership and uniformity. Their answer to this problem was to "PROFESSIONALISE" the rural brigades.

24

Powell must have known what was afoot because in 1939 he requested to be appointed as a salaried chief officer. The council refused. Even after all the preparation and ground work he had carried out in respect of improving the Brigades efficiency.

Powell had documented the needs of the Brigade in respect of the 1938 act stating that it took 1 minute to "turn out" from receipt of a fire call and the furthest point was 6 miles, which would take 8½ minutes to reach. He recommend a centralised training establishment at Hitchin. Emergency trailer pumps had already been issued to auxillary firemen at St Ippolytts, Holwell, Hexton, Kings Walden, Langley, Offley, Lilley, St. Pauls Walden, Pirton, Preston, & the Wymondley's.

These areas were covered by Hitchin and C.O. Powell considered that these auxillaries need training before working with the "original volunteers".

The equipment on the Hitchin Fire station in 1938 was ÷ 1/ The 40 H.P Leyland, with 1500 feet of hose, Foam generator, 2 oxygen breathing apparatus sets, 1 pure air set, an extension ladder, a scaling ladder, a jump sheet, a 100 foot manilla line.

2/ The Morris Guy, with davy escape line.

3/ Spare equipment ÷ one scaling ladder, 30 foot extension ladder.

The staff at the station was ÷ 3 officers, 1 engineer, & 15 fully trained firemen. The additional equipment required by C.F.O; Powell was another engine, to replace the Morris Guy. It would have a 500 g.p.m pump. Also a large trailer pump and a 2 ton 26 h.p. tender. He also asked for 4 extra men. His requests were supported by the fact that Hitchin were called to more incidents than Letchworth, Baldock, Royston, & Welwyn Garden City put together.

A Fire Brigade committee was formed within the council to make decisions that related solely to fire brigade matters, and women were invited to the annual dinner for the first time. Their comments when asked were, "I THINK YOUR FIREMEN ARE WONDERFUL".

1938 was reported to be the "most active year in the Brigades experience" Air raid precaution drills were arranged with the Stevenage, Royston & Letchworth Brigades and provision was made for a possible 30 fires per mile in the class A risk area. Chemical and gas warfare were included in the preparations also.

44 calls were made on the Brigade in 1938, and whereas only 20 years previously the calls had been predominently farms and stacks they were now to residential property. Of the 44 calls, 41 had been actual fires including 16 houses, 3 shops, 2 motor cars, 2 factories, 1 school room, 1 storeshed, a Garage & a Public house. Along with these there was 7 stacks, 3 grass fires & 2 fences. 1 malicious call and 1 false alarm.

Powell resigned in 1939, following the councils refusal of his application to be a paid Chief Officer. It was suggested at the time that he was going because he had not obey Home office instructions to recruit an extra 14 men and only recruited 7, thereby saving the ratepayers £21 a week.

Powell the gentleman to the end, asked his men to give their loyalty to their new Chief officer.

ollowing Powells resignation, the position of Chief Officer was filled by Station Officer Clarke of the Luton Brigade, a professional fireman by trade. He in turn was replaced in 1940 by C.O. Kehoe. Clarke and Kehoe were not Hitchin men as all their predecessors had been, and the "true" volunteer chief officer had ended with Powell. This situation was redressed in 1941, to some degree, when "Ernie" Reynolds (one of C.F.O. Jacob Reynolds sons) was made Company Officer in the newly formed National Fire Service.. Company Officer Reynolds was one of the pre-war volunteers and was in charge of the main station in Paynes Park and two satellite stations, one in Grove Road and another in Sun street.

These stations relied on local traders with their lorries to haul the trailer pumps with which they had been issued. Such named traders as, French, Turner, Griffin, & Franklin used their lorries to pull the Scammel & Coventry Climax pumps. The area was covered by several of the old brigades amalgamated into area 12, Hitchin being in C division

NFS
12

1941~48

Each satellite station was crewed by 5 watches with an average of 6 men per watch. One watch was detailed as the regional crew, and they could then be detailed to attend anywhere in the country at a moments notice. Their families were never informed and these firemen could be away for days at a time, to such places as, Manchester, Thames Haven and Purfleet, and of course London. These targets when hit required many appliances. It was on one of these convoys that Fireman LOVATI a Hitchin fireman was accidently killed by the Letchworth auxillary appliance at a stop-over at Newmarket Chase.

In the town itself there were at least 29 organised pumping sites, including plank dams, rivers and ornamental ponds. At the sewage works in Burymead Road there was the purification lagoon containing 100,000 gallons of water. On Butts Close a brick surface tank contained 25,000 gallons, & in the Market square there was a similar surface tank.

The Morris Guy was last used in 1939 and was replaced by a Bedford. Kehoe had modified an Albion bus, which carried its own dam and pump. It was much admired and was featured in in the Fire magazine of the day. Again the "regular" ~ Russells Tannery caught fire in 1940 and once more in 1941, damage incurred was respectively £4000 & £17000.

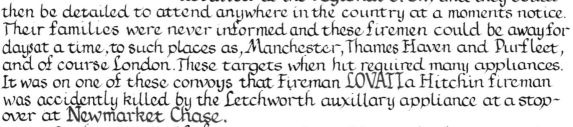

The Albion Coach designed & built by C.F.O. Kehoe & the Hitchin A.F.S. It was a brand new vehicle, commandeered from Maidment garages

Hitchin was not without incident during this conflict, over 100 high explosive bombs were dropped and numerous incendiaries and oil bombs were dropped throughout the town and rural areas, keeping the N.F.S. busy. Leading Fireman Whittenburys' instructions during an air raid were to shelter under the railway bridge in Grove Road. Considering that railways and bridges were prime targets, It would appear that there was great confidence in the inability of the enemy bomb aimers.

26

When in September 1944 a flying bomb crashed on Pirton, destroying cottages and the local N.F.S accomodation, it was claimed to be the fastest turn out ever, as they were literally blown out of their beds by the explosion! The 18th July 1944 and West End Farm, Offley, was hit by a Lancaster bomber returning from a raid. It flattened the house, killing Mrs Handley and two of her family. The crew of eight were also killed, and the aircraft ignited. Hitchin with Rickmansworth attended. Along with the flying bomb incident it was probably felt by the firemen that nothing worse could happen. In this they were wrong. In January 1945, at Offley once again, an american lorry laden with bombs, skidded on icy roads and collided with a bus outside of Glebe Farm. The lorries petrol tank ignited in a 30 foot sheet of flame. The american driver managed to

A Wartime trailer pump towed by a "private car".

warn the occupants of Glebe Farm, who were lucky to escape with their lives, as considerable damage was caused when the bombs exploded. When Hitchin arrived they found that 7 people were killed, 18 injured, cattle were burned and hay stacks had been set alight.

The competition drills were still taking, although on a larger scale. Hitchin hosted the 1944 event, which was held on Ransoms recreation ground. Although not operation-al "firemen" as such, the womens complement of the Hitchin brigade entered a team.

In 1946 one of the stalwarts of the old volunteer brigade died. Ex~Chief Officer Jacob Reynolds. One of Logsdons men, he had, like the other chiefs risen through the ranks. He was 70 years old when he died at his public house, the Highlander. Only one of the volunteer Chief officers was left ~ Powell.

July of the same year, and the Brigade were kept busy, answering 4 fire calls in 24 hours. One in Bearton Road saw 5 G.P.O vehicles destroyed at a large garage fire. The road had recently been tarmaced, and the hydrant was stuck tight. It was fortunate that a water tender attended. Within the same period the Brigade were called to an ammunition dump at Clophill and the old A.R.P. hut at the rear of the fire station.

With the war now behind them, and much to the annoyance of the urban council, the government in 1947 revealed their plan to return the Brigades not to local councils, but to the County Councils. This brought howls of protest throughout the council ranks. Statements were made by the chairman, Mr. King and councill-ors Chenery, Saunders & Foster, who said it "was putting the clock back 51 years. The worst affront was that Hitchin was placed lower in importance than Bishops Stortford, Ware & Hertford, and it was ludicrous to suggest that Hitchin could be manned by 12 men. After all, they had 3 permanent staff & 16 volunteers in 1939, and had answered 50 calls that year!"

The Fire Brigade Badge 1948

The government were not to be too concerned by the local councils arguments, and on the 1st APRIL 1948 "FROM THE ASHES OF THE NATIONAL FIRE SERVICE", Chief Fire Officer Geoffrey Blackstone George Medal & C.B.E assumed command of THE HERTFORDSHIRE FIRE AND AMBULANCE BRIGADE and Hitchin was no longer under control of the Town hall, the end of an 134 year association.

27

Blackstone called for 400 volunteers and 230 came forward. It was proposed to have 4 full time men at Hitchin, and Letchworth was to become the control station. The cost to the Hertfordshire County Council of the Brigade was £91052 per year, equal to a 7½ᵈ rate. By then Hitchins' population had risen to 25000. Company Officer Ralph French became the first and only retained Station Officer at Hitchin. Also in 1948 E.S.A at Stevenage was severely damaged by fire, once again, calling on 8 brigades for assistance, one of which was Hitchin. In July of the same year Thompsons Garage in Queen Street was damaged by fire to the tune of £15000~£20000. The fire also spread to the laundry, damaging the roof. Letchworth & Baldock assisted Hitchin. All were commended for a job well done, including water engineer Stanley Davey (son of ex-C.F.O. J. Davey) and an ex-volunteer fireman himself.

The appliance situation was in some disarray in 1948, and Hitchin received an ex-Loughton appliance, A Dennis Ace "New World appliance. It was originally sent to Hertfordshire to be used as spares but fireman Waldock at Letchworth made it serviceable. As it was to replace the Leyland F.E.1. which had given nearly 20 years service, but on which the firemen had to ride on the outside compared to riding "inboard" on the Dennis, it was said, that firemen no longer had to, "Stand in fear of their lives", as they had on the Leyland.

In 1949 water mains were to be installed between Lilley & Hexton, and Offley and Pirton, and Fireman Rogers became the "Rain Nymph", supplying "rain" for the film set of, No Place for Jennifer, filmed at Lyles Row Hitchin.

C.F.O. Blackstone in 1950 was having a running battle with the local councils, especially Hitchin, trying to explain that Hitchin had cost £4383 to run, whereas in 1937 it had only cost £776, and referring to inflation he claimed that an ounce of tobacco only cost 8ᵈ in 1938. He went on to explain that a fire-mans wages in 1937 was £3, in 1950 £7. A fire engine in 1937~£2000, in 1950 £4750. All of the 470 ball hydrants installed in 1830, had been replaced, at a cost of £10350~9/3, and two new ones had cost £71. This did not appease the council who voted 7~3 to demand "THEIR" brigade back, due to the "economic way they had run it". They were not successful in their demand.

The ambulance brigade had been placed under the control of the fire brigade following the reorganisation. The station at Paynes Park was to be their accomodation. They were soon to receive the Daimler ambulances, a purpose built vehicle. Reputed to be the finest ambulance ever and never surpassed.

The Dennis Ace "New World appliance 1947/8. Reg.No DPu 16

The Daimler Ambulance c.1950

28

In 1951 & 52 respectively Hitchin experienced two large fires, said to be spectacular. The first in 1951 at the Hitchin Glove factory in Burymead Road, where the building was gutted. Hitchin and Letchworth firemen fought the flames for five hours, whilst a great pall of smoke covered Hitchin.

The latter fire in 1952 occurred at Arnotts Productions, printers and bookbinders in Sun Street, the area of highest fire risk in Hitchin, with predominently common roof voids and timber construction through-out both Sun Street and Bucklesbury. By the time Hitchin arrived on the scene the fire was "blazing through the roof". The Hitchin crew attacked the blaze from Sun St; and when Letchworth arrived with their pump and salvage tender they "got to work" in Bucklesbury. At the height of the blaze there was some concern at the possible involvement of Barhams explosive store and Newtons yard, with its combustible building materials. A bitter irony indeed, con-

Fm Ernie Reynolds & Fm Ralph French c 1933 Both destined to become O/c of Hitchin Fire Brigade

sidering the amount of fires in this area that these two long dead Chief officers had dealt with. The fire was con-tained, but not before several valuable first editions were destroyed, and sadly four volumes of the handwritten Venice Bible, in Hebrew.

In February 1952 the Sun Hotel, so much a part of the fire brigades history was sold for £19500 and a man was arrested for stealing 3 gallons of petrol from a fire brigade vehicle at Paynes Park. He was fined £25.

101 fires were attended in 1952 by the Hitchin Brigade, a massive increase compared to the 8^s & 12^s of previous years.

1953 saw the first proposal of the Priory-by-pass, which finally became a reality in 1981.

Hitchin was now one of the 33 stations making the Hertford-shire Fire Brigade. The county was split into two divisions, east and west. Hitchin became a number, ~9. The wholetime fireman occupying the flat above the fire station now, was Leading fireman Guyton. Later to become Deputy Chief Fire Officer of the Hertfordshire Fire Brigade.

The war time appliances were gradually being replaced. The old Bedford being replaced by a 'Green Goddess'. This in turn being replaced by an 'S' type Bedford.

The Green Goddess

In early 1954, the former home of De Vere Doughty, Ickleford Manor caught fire. It was now the property of Ward & Ward, a London chemical company. Of the 25 rooms in danger, 8 were saved by the efforts of the firemen from Hitchin, Letchworth, Stevenage & Shefford stations. The thatched roof and one wing of the building was destroyed. The villagers helped the firemen to lift water from the river, when hyd-rant pressure found to be insufficient. A matter that water engineer Davey soon rectified.

29

Arson then was still the plague to firefighters that it always has been. 5 fires in 24 hours occurred in March 1955. Not all fire-raisers escaped capture, as demonstrated when "BOSUN" the police dog tracked one Fred Shard 5 miles across country, where he was then arrested for lighting two stacks in Gosmore!

On new years day 1956 the children attending the annual party at Victaulics in Wilbury Way, received an unexpected surprise when fire broke out on the premises. For them a memor--able way to start the year.

Sadly Linda Mary Ann Browne, 3½ years old of Mattocke road became the victim of the other side of fire, when her dress caught fire whilst dancing in front of the fire at her home in November 1956.

The Angels Vaults, the home of many of the annual firemans dinners of so many years earlier was demolished and another tie to the old Brigade was severed. 1957 and Station Officer Ralph French was married, he was to die only one year later. He was accorded a fire--mans funeral and buried alongside the boundary wall of the St: Johns road cemetery. By a strange coincidence the same wall also became the bound-ary wall of the new fire station in 1967 and not more than a few yards from his grave lay Edwin Logsdon, one of his predecessors. During his service Stn.Off: French had led the retained force and was one of only seven retained men to receive the coronation medal.

The Angels Vaults

There was at this time great difficulty recruiting retained men due to new housing being so far away, and the cost of running the Brigade was increasing every year. From £700 on the old scheme to a staggering £5000 in 1957. A point stressed by Cllr: Hill in 1959 who said, " the cost of the Fire Brigade was shocking compared to the previous method of running it"

When the original home of the fire brigade was set on fire in 1958 by an arsonist, so large was the blaze at Newtons yard that four pumps were required to contain the blaze. C.F.O Blackstone himself attended. Following several instances of fire within the town by the arsonist (who by now had modernised his approach by using firelighters!) he finally selected the "old fire station". 1250 gallons of water per minute were pumped onto the fire by the Hitchin, Baldock & Stevenage pumps. The heat was so intense that firemen were reported as having been "sunburned". The historic "tithe barn" nearby was saved, and a nearby house evacuated as a precaution. £5000 of damage was caused. Water engineer Davey was once again on hand, if his

The Coronation Medal, struck in silver.

services were required. This would be one of the last occasions, as the water company was soon to be absorbed in the Lea Valley Group.

30

The following year, 1959 saw Brookers new showroom severely damaged by fire, necessitating four jets. The cause, a faulty flourescent light fitting. The 5 pumps attending took 1 hour to bring the fire under control. The damage could have been a lot worse if it had not been spotted by David Payne, a Paternoster newspaper boy & Tom Brooker an ex-fireman. Brookers shop was not the only business to have serious fire damage averted by the efforts of the Hitchin Firemen & their colleagues from neighbouring stations, Wm Ransoms experienced their first fire since their establishment in 1846. It started in shavings and spread too rapidly for employees to deal with. The firemen stopped the spread and avoided a serious fire and explosive situation.

At the annual dinner, which had once again been resurrected the year before, along with Don Powell, Harry Cannon and Ernie Reynolds, the "old hands" were privileged to have as their main guest C.F.O. Blackstone. Also the oldest surviving member of the old Brigade Alec Seymour was present. No doubt as the evening stretched on, so did the stories!!

C.F.O.
Don Powell
1930

A taste of what was in store, now that the local councils were being freed from their responsibilities for the fire brigade appeared in 1960, when the town council gave the county council 18 months notice that lease on the old fire station would not be renewed. Cllr. T. Brooker saw no reason why a fire station should be on a main road! Cllr Thake was the only one who was against this proposal, on the grounds, "that Hitchin might lose its fire station completely with this approach" (A not unknown occurrence, as this happened to Letchworth in 1980, although for different reasons)

Unrest was creeping into the Brigade in 1961, demonstrations in parliament square by the full time fireman over their wages and conditions of service, did not at this time affect the Hitchin Firemen, being retained. The A.F.S was to finish shortly due to compulsory retirement of the wartime men and a lack of recruits due to the long hours, poor wages & risk was affecting the whole brigade.

The retained competitions were still taking place. In 1962 Hitchin entered 2 teams, the 'B' team made up of, LFm Whittenbury, Fm Cannon, Fm. Bullen Fm Smith, Fm. Hilton, tied with the Baldock team for 1st. place in a time of 29⅗ seconds. The 'A' team made up of, LFm Grant, Fm Abbiss, Fm. Huthwaite, Fm Springett & Fm. Tilley took 3rd place in 30 seconds.

The "Dinky Toy" 555 MRO

Stations neighbouring Hitchin had over the last few years been getting new appliances, and in 1963 Hitchin finally received theirs, a Bedford Miles water tender ladder (35 foot) reg No. 555 MRO , affectionately called "the Dinky toy" it replaced the auxillary pump.

31

On May 10th 1963 Herbert Barham died, the man whom it was said had bought the old steamer in 1929 for £10! *(Current value of a steam appliance in 1986 ≈ £20000!)* He joined the Brigade at the age of 13 and was so small, a special uniform had to be made for him. He was 75 years of age. Hugh Cannon, another ex "brigadier" followed him shortly after, at the age of 65.

On the lighter side, the Brigade were called to the home of Mrs Florence Braybrook at 43 The Avenue. Mrs Braybrook was an eccentric lady to say the least, and every room within her house bar one, was full of junk. Prams, bikes, coal weights, books from floor to ceiling & even a complete bar from a Public house. It literally took the Firemen hours to make inroads into the building to ensure the fire was out.

A fire in the lounge of the Arcadia Hotel in Walsworth Road in February 1965. Led to 6 people being rescued from the window ledge by the Hitchin Firemen and 3 youths being led to safety through the smoke.

The wages of the Hitchin firemen consisted of a retaining fee and payments for turning out on the appliance or standing by at the station of 21/3 & 11/3 respectively. *(1/3 old currency is equivalent to 5p. 1988 rates for turn outs & standing by are £7·20 &£3·91).* The new fire station had again been mooted in 1965, a trifle longer than the 18 months notice given in 1960.

Two old 'stagers' made their "LAST SHOUT" in 1966. Harry Cannon in January, and the last volunteer Chief Officer Don Powell, the thespian and excellent bass voice singer, who had given pleasure with his songs on many an annual dinner.

In the same year Brookers fertiliser store became a blazing inferno, which the Brigade soon tamed and SIR GEORGE ABBISS a Pirton resident and inventor of the 999 system of emergency calls died.

When fire bombs were put through the letter box of Mr Geraldi, a sicilian gentleman living in Bearton Road he stated, "he was certain it had nothing to do with the mafia"

The new station in Newtons Way was topped out on the 22nd, September 1967. It had cost £175000 to build and comprised a 4 bay station for fire and ambulance vehicles. The station was built on the day manning principal with accomodation for the 12 firemen built around the fire station.

32

It is custom when the last brick is laid at a topping out ceremony that all present have a glass of beer in their hand. Present at the ceremony were C.F.O Blackstone, G.M, CBE. Divisional Officer Cotton, Deputy Div. Off: Reynolds, Assistant Div: Off: Briars, Assistant Chief Officer Hughes, Chief insp: Mynott, Stevenage police, Inspector Hilton & sgt: Wade, Hitchin police, Cllr: Saunders, the chairman of the County council, Mr. Wilson, clerk, and Mr. King, surveyor. When the party arrived at the top of the 57 foot tower Blackstone said, "THIS IS SERIOUS, THERE IS NO BEER UP HERE! SEND UP THE BEER". After the ceremony the ¾ full keg was left for the workmen on the following day. It has been ascertained that firemen on duty that evening RESCUED the barrel and the fluid in it, before returning a somewhat lighter barrel to the tower roof before morning. The station was finally ready for occupation on February 9th. 1968. Because of difficulties experienced housing the new Bedford water tender escape, VAR 107 E that Hitchin now possessed within the old station. ~ The firemen, who had already occupied their houses in Newtons Way were allowed to take the escape appliance home at night and park it by the incomplete new station. When a fire call was received at Paynes Park the watchroom man actuated a telephone specially installed on the wall outside 11 Newtons Way. Hoping that one of the sleeping firemen would answer it!

Newtons Way 1968.

The old station in Paynes Park (*demolished in 1988*) held many memories for some of the firemen. Once during a drill period, which was apparently so realistic, that a member of the public rushed up and snatched the hose from Fireman Bateman, saying, "he would help". Much to the delight of the aforementioned and the fury of the officer in charge.

When Hitchin became a day manning station, the reliance on the towns-men for the fire brigade was substantially reduced over--night. Now the town had a paid professional Brigade. To the retained men, relegated to the second appliance, if required, it was a bitter pill to swallow.

Bedford T.R. Escape 1967.
V.A.R. 107 E.

When the station became "full time" it was deemed necessary to appoint a supervisory officer to maintain the smooth running of the station. This post, taken by Station Officer R. Ambrose was to last until 1973. During this period there were three station officers, inclusive of Ambrose.

33

When Fireman Henry Terry finally retired after 29 years service in 1968, it was the end of an era, as he was one of the last original volunteer firemen still serving. He had enlisted for military service at the outbreak of war, only to be called back by Chief Officer Kehoe during the 'blitz'. He was eventually returned to the forces and on demobilisation he joined the retained service. (At the time of writing, 1988. Ex-Leading Fireman Whittenbury & Fireman Terry still often visit the fire station for a drink and a "yarn".) In 1948 the mobilising control responsible for Hitchin had been Letchworth. It was then passed to Stevenage and in 1970 to Hertford which it still is to this day. The siren and house bells for so long the call to duty for firemen were replaced by pocket radio alerters. The 'good ship Danaë' was "scuttled" by fire *(The sea cadets training establishment in Bedford Road) in 1969, with rifles and ammunition the only things saved. A Mrs Olga Hamilton jumped from her first floor window in Garden Row when her oil stove ignited and a house in Chalkdell Path blew up just after firemen had left having investigated an earlier call. Walls, roof, doors and windows collapsed onto Dorothy & Percy Morgan, it was believed to be an electrical surge that was responsible, as sparks had been seen in a cupboard of nearby number 38, earlier.

Station Officer Ron Ambrose c 1967

Mrs Ada McKenzie of 5 High Dane died when her dressing gown caught fire as did Henrietta Worledge of New Crown Cottages, West Street, Lilley. Despite an heroic attempt by Mr Alec McDonald to save her.

An intimation of forthcoming events was to be seen, by the work to rule of firemen in 1970, but as yet those events were in the future.

On Friday 8th September 1971, a nightmare to all firemen occurred, when, in the London Road, a fully laden petrol tanker overturned at the junction of Sunnyside Road. Thousands of gallons of petrol poured down the hill towards the junction of Whitehill and Stevenage Road. The driver Mr Anthony Smith from Basildon attempted to escape from his cab as the petrol exploded, but died in the inferno. The Firemen were praised for their courage, When at the risk of further explosions "they stood and did their job". For the new station officer, Hugh Wheeler, who had only taken command of Hitchin in August, it must have been a real "baptism by fire".

Tanker, Junction of Stevenage Road & Sunnyside Road 1971

In 1972 Fireman Miller had a close shave with death when at Bowmans mill, chlorine gas escaped. His breathing apparatus face mask became dislodged, in atmosphere where 1 cubic foot of chlorine in 1000 cubic feet of air is enough to kill. Coffee mornings were started at the fire station, where home made cakes and toys would be sold for xmas presents for children.

The working week of the firemen had been reduced from 80 hours to 56 hours and would remain so until 1975 when they would be further reduced to 48 hours. Fire prevention was now being strongly imposed following the 1971 fire precautions act. The Cock, Lister & Highbury Lodge hotels were all threatened with immediate closure and court proceedings if they did not comply with the act. The firemen at Hitchin were called upon to undertake fire prevention duties in the form of the Office, Shop & railway premise act 1963. This necessitated the firemen visiting businesses within the town and rural areas to inspect the extinguishers and means of escape. All the fire prevention

Carry down.

in the world would not have stopped 7 year old Christopher Doolan climbing a 33000 volt electricity pylon in St. Michaels mount on the 16th April 1973. He fell 30 feet, burning from the waist down. He was rescued by Sub officer Sullivan, but he had sustained very serious burns. And full evacuation of mothers and babies was called for at North Herts Maternity hospital in Bedford road on the 8th August 1973, when the bedding store in the basement caught fire, filling the building with smoke. This proved to be a very difficult breathing apparatus job.

Stn Officer Carbin.

After 2 years service as officer in charge of the Hitchin "brigade", Station Officer Wheeler was posted to Moreton in the Marsh, Glos: the Home Office training establishment. His place was taken by Station Officer K. Carbin, an ex London fireman, he had earned a commendation for rescuing a drowning child and had attended fires at Buckingham Palace and Bishopsgate.

1974 saw the only recorded rescue by escape ladder at Hitchin. When Mr. Ernest James was trapped on a 3rd floor balcony by smoke from a fire within his flat.

he ambulance service were to leave Hitchin Fire Station for good on the 27th. November 1974. Their new base at Letchworth Gate, was under the command of John Sweetman, an ex-fireman who had occupied the flat over the old station in Paynes Park. And at a large fire in December 1974 at Redhill "Autos" the Brigade gave Mr. Edward Bell a "christmas present" when they saved "his pride & joy ~ A 1906 TRICYCLE. The fire caused the Firs hotel to be evacuated and lorries in Deamers depot to be moved. A 6000 gallon diesel oil tank was also in danger of becoming involved ~ but Mr Bell's tricycle was saved.

Meanwhile the Hitchin Firemen had been issued with a Dennis Jaguar appliance to replace the "dinky toy". It was fitted with a "crash" gearbox, CRASH being the operative word! With the blessing of their divisional commander, Peter Reid they exchanged it for a second hand Dennis Rolls Royce automatic. A branch mans nightmare as if the pump operator was "heavy hand" with the pump controls the motor would automatically change down a gear, lifting the branchman clear off the ground, resulting in a string

1969 Dennis Rolls automatic.

of expletives describing the questionable parenthood of said pump operator! This appliance was later to catch fire in a corn field at Breachwood Green during the exceptional summer of 1976. It was only saved by the determined efforts of the crew from total destruction.

1975, and a fire at the British Oxyen caused the largest amount of cylinders ever on one site to explode. Although at Dunhams Lane, Letchworth; Hitchin were part of the first attendance. Exploding cylinders, it was reported "were taking off like rockets and fragmenting as they exploded. Pieces of cylinder being found considerable dist~ ~ance away, as it was said were some of the FIREMEN!"

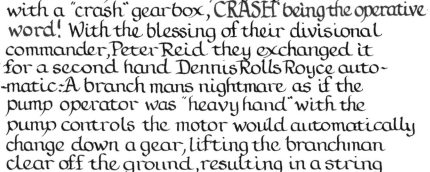

Retained L/Fm Don Lilley.

Industrial action over the London "weighting allowance" brought the Brigade once more into a "Go slow" dispute. The Firemen at Hitchin were expelled from the union for not obeying a union instr~ ~uction to hand in their "bleepers".

36

In the same year, 1975, 25 firemen from Hitchin and Stevenage along with 2 police officers whilst answering a call to a chemical incident at Walkern, drove straight into a cloud of the chemical ~ Anhydrous Ammonia. They were all taken to Lister hospital for check ups. Although not a dangerous substance on this occasion, it gave cause for concern.

December 18th 1975, saw an incident that shocks even fire~ ~men, and brings home the lesson "that speed kills". A Ford Escort motor car whilst negotiating the bend by the bridge at Little Wymondley, with the driver "using his racing skills" struck an on~ ~coming Citroen car. The Ford overturned and burst into flames. 3 of the occupants died, 2 were burned to death & 1 died later from burns (Victor Page, William Hogarth & Alan Stephen) The one survivor was rescued by Jeff Askew, an off duty police officer.

The Fire Service Benevolent fund is a national charity that cares for widows and orphans of Firemen. It relies on voluntary donations and the endeavours of the firemen themselves to raise money. Each station has its own benevolent representative. The Hitchin 'rep' was Fireman Alan Patmore, who by his efforts and cajouling of the other firemen held several open days at Hitchin, The like of which had not been seen within the Brigade. The wives and families were all involved, and by the generosity of the towns people and other visitors, several thousand pounds was raised.

The "new" Brigade Logo, adopted in the mid seventies

It was something of a surprise when Hitchins old "Dennis Ace" resurfaced in virtually pristine condition, the owner looking for somewhere to store it. Patmore sensing a good benevolent asset took responsibility for it and used it during its stay at Hitchin for many fund raising functions. The trans~ ~portation of the carol singing firemen around the Hitchin 'pubs' at Christmas, and the carriage of two of the Firemens daughters, Jill Golding and Heather Sibley to their weddings. Along with the "Monster piano smash" in 1976 when £373 was raised, the stations efforts were finally recognised and Hitchin were awarded a diploma for its magnificent efforts by the area committee.

37

Station Officers at Hitchin were now a thing of the past. Carbin having left in 1975, The station now being run by two Sub. officers, Sullivan and Dolan. Early in 1976 Sullivan retired, having held the officer in charge position on three occasions at Hitchin. His place was taken by Sub. officer A. Lemm (both of Sub.o. Lemms sons were later to become retained. Along with retained L-fireman Huthwaite & his two sons, once again making strong family ties in the towns Brigade, as previously existed with the Barham & Reynolds families.)

On the 12th March 1976 the Brigade were called to "PERSONS REPORTED" in a fire at No 2 Austage End, a small remote hamlet. The Hitchin crews who had been at work most of the night on a magnesium swarf fire at Williams scrap yard, Wallace Way, had just been relieved by a Stevenage pump and were on their way back to the station when the call was received. On arrival and already fatigued, they found that they had to run ½ mile uphill from the nearest hydrant to fight the inferno that confronted them. The building collapsed having been burning for several hours. There was no hope for Mrs Jessie Allock, the old lady perished in the flames.

Sub. officer A. Lemm.

In May 1976 the Hitchin Court in Bancroft was 'fired' by an arsonist. A difficult and dangerous fire to bring under control. The No.2 courtroom was severely damaged by fire. The arsonist, apprehended in September of the same year, probably never knew how lucky he was not to have been charged with a much more serious crime, as at one stage the court clerk was lost in the smoke filled building, unbeknown to the firemen. Fortunately he found his way out to safety.

1976 & 77 were two of the hottest summers recorded, over 100 calls were answered by Hitchin in one month. Some calls as far as Bramfield forest in Hertford. At one stage water rationing was considered in Hertfordshire. The Green Goddesses were brought out of mothball to supplement the overstretched machines and crews. This proved to be a very fortuitous move, considering events that were to occur in 1977.

Retained L-fm Paul Huthwaite

32 crop fires occurred in 14 days during At Easthall farm the Hitchin Firemen had to "run a gauntlet of flames" to reach the seat of the fire, and Arthur Morris died of asphyxiation due to smoke in a fire at the Fox public house Darley Hall.

38

1977 started with a bang for the Hitchin Firemen, when on the 2nd. January a car carrying 200 shotgun cartridges caught fire in the Cambridge road. The result of which was a TREMENDOUS EXPLOSION; and Fusilier Graham Waugh leapt off of a train whilst returning to barracks when he saw a fire in the Technofinish factory at Cadwell Lane. He was given £100 reward for his attempts at extinguishing the fire before the arrival of the Brigade. Also the first of several light aircraft crashes that the Hitchin firemen experienced occurred at the Lawrence End estate, near Breachwood Green in February of that year.

By now the escape ladders were becoming an expensive comm--odity, especially when requiring repairs. They were therefore being replaced. Much to the annoyance of the "old escape men", Which included all of the Hitchin Firemen, who between the 18 of them had approx: 325 years service. This could not be match ed anywhere in the country. The appliance that replaced the BEDFORD escape was a Dodge, carrying a 45 foot ladder, also having hose laying facilities, high pressure hose reels and a 1000 gallon per minute pump.

Dodge (Perkins) with 45' ladder. SG6 864 R.

100 years had seen a lot of difference, but not much improvement. The ladder was tortuous in application, and the rearward facing crew seats caused nausea among the firemen.

The current cost of running the Hertfordshire Fire Brigade was £3800000 and expected to rise to £4 million. This did not stop the union demanding a massive 30% pay rise for the firemen. This was refused by the employers, and in November 1977 the first national strike by the fire brigade started. Swept along with the powerful metropolitan brigades, the rural brigades had no option but to comply. Hitchin to a man stayed on duty during the nine weeks of the strike, as they were not members of the union. This did not endear them to their union colleagues. But all Hitchin Firemen were now residents of the town and were just as parochial as were their predecessors. Needless to say Hitchin Firemen were "BLACKED". The Green Goddess appliances was brought out of 'mothball' and crewed by regular soldiers who had been given very basic training. Their pumps were located at local police stations. They were commanded by a fire brigade officer.

The 45 foot Aluminium extending ladder (13.5 m)

39

Although the soldiers efforts at firefighting were commendable, they did not possess the expertise of professional firemen. Needless to say due to a lack of large incidents during this period they held the fire service together until the end of the strike in early 1978. There was much animosity within the Brigade, not only directed at the Hitchin firemen but also within all ranks throughout the service. Many firemen to this day say it was the undoing of the fire service, even when taking into account the 22% pay award and the reduction in hours to 42 per week. However, time heals, and gradually the Brigade returned to normal.

The year started off with a major fire at Kings Walden on the Sir Thomas Pilkington estate, when the village post office, store and adjoining property were virtually destroyed by fire. Mr. Dennis Hopper and shopkeeper Paul Phillips and their families were made homeless. Unfortunately Mr Phillips while running to raise the alarm had a heart attack and was taken to hospital. Later the villagers had a collection for the families and raised £1078. One local "character" raffled his transistor radio at the Sportsmans public house, Stopsley and raised £31=25p!

Retained Fireman David Lenin.

Also in the first months of the year a serious fire occurred at the Sikh temple in Radcliffe Road, where no amount of persuasion could get the worshippers to leave even though it was smoke "logged", and firemen wearing breathing apparatus were hauling hose through the temple.

Meanwhile Sub-officer Dolan and Fireman Patmore were taking the county council to an industrial tribunal under the "EQUAL PAY ACT 1970 & THE SEX DISCRIMINATION ACT" over the difference in wages between themselves and retained firemen which included two women firefighters stationed at Much Hadham; they put a good case but finally lost.

Fm Reg Bateman

In June 1978 Hitchins only "fireboat" The HIZ (a model) was launched on the pond outside the fire station. The pond built by Fireman Bateman soon after the station was opened was meant to be a "small" pond. Having obtained permission from the officer in charge, Stn. Officer Ambrose, Fireman Bateman set to work!

40

When the station officer returned from his holiday. He found the front of the station transformed. Several tons of soil had been dug out and in its place were two ponds on different levels. One was 25 feet by 12 feet and the other one was 12 feet by 7 feet! It was so big that Fireman Brown organised a Hitchin Fire station fishing team and a 2½ pound Chubb was later quite comfortably installed. The pond and garden were a credit to the firemen who maintained them; Firemen Wickham and Wareham, and brought many compliments from visiting Home office inspectors.

The farmers within the area, as they were nationally, were coming under increasing pressure to restrict the practice of stubble burning. During the late summer the Brigade were inundated with calls to stubble fires 'out of control', highways were being obliter-ated by smoke, causing traffic accidents. Dirt and ash was blown for miles. Finally along with the cooperation of The National Farmers union the government tightened up the laws in respect of stubble burning.

Fm Gordon Brown

On Monday 5th December 1978, FATIMA KHATOON died at her home in York Road, due to a fire. She was only 19 months old. This incident was dealt with by the Royston crew, whilst the Hitchin crew were at Stevenage being drilled by their divisional officer.

January 1979 saw U.F.O.s reported over the area. One might attribute the fire in the INLAND REVENUE OFFICE Bancroft to them, but it was more likely to have been arson as was the fire at Hawkins the Solicitors; at the same time. £20000 of damage was done by fire at The Hitchin Post restaurant in Hermitage road, caused by a chip pan. Breathing apparatus was essential now on most incidents. Long gone were the days of the SMOKE EATERS. Toxic gases 'given off' by 'modern' materials when on fire, were recognised for the damage they caused to the firemens health. 1979 also saw Welbury School at Offley damaged by fire, when a paraffin heater set fire to the gymnasium. This time the Hitchin crews stopped the fire spread, mainly due to the modern appliances carrying a water supply of their own. A facility C.F.O. Powell never had on the Leyland F.E.1, forty six years earlier, when they lost a great deal of the building.

Fm. Dennis Wickham.

41

With the severe floods that were to occur in 1980, Fireman Arthur Golding may well have rued the day that he shewed his certificate of merit to the press from Queen Juliana of the Neder~lands, in recognition of the work carried out during the 1950 Dutch floods when he was a national serviceman. Hitchin was to be extensively flooded, especially in the Bridge street area, where water was rushing up the drains. The Hitchin Firemen were helpless. The council were forced by the residents to undertake extensive improvements to the drains in the area, especially when having just dried out from the first deluge it happened again.

On cup-final day of the same year HIGH PRAISE was given to the Hitchin Firemen by the headmaster of the Hitchin High school, when they successfully extinguished a major fire in one of classrooms, with the minimum amount of damage, mainly due to the use of high pressure hose reels. When a second fire was found it be~came obvious that arson was once again respon~sible.

Once again the year ended with a tragedy. Mrs. Beatrice Rowe Gillett, 77 years of age, burn~ed to death in her bed at Salusbury Lane, Offley and Mrs. Evelyn Danahar, 63 years of age of Chaucer Way was rescued by the Fire~men from her burning property, only to die several days later.

Retained Fm Andrew Lemm

1980 was a relatively quiet year except for the floods already mentioned and a blazing ammunition lorry that overturned on the A1 motorway. Fortunately it was late at night and the motorway was closed while 3000 rounds of ammunition exploded. The 2nd of September saw the labor~atories of Ickleford Manor seriously damaged by fire, warranting six appliances including a pump from Shefford. The fire was suspected to be Arson. A suspicion well justified when in 1981 the same laboratory was "fired" again, calling for five appliances, £100,000 damage was caused, nearly twice as much as the first fire.

Retained Fm Glen Favrey.

It may be difficult to apprehend the arsonist, but thieves are another matter, when in February 1980 two Royston Firemen, Leading Fireman Johnson and Fireman Sharpe whilst walking through Hitchin gave chase to a jewel thief, who had robbed a shop in the churchyard. He was relentlessly pursued as far as Chalkdell path where he was caught by Leading Fireman Johnson.

ire calls were dropping in 1981 according to statistics. But varied emergencies still occurred with regular frequency. Such an emergency happened when a LOCKHEED JETSTAR aircraft crashed into the landing lights at Luton Airport. The odd thing about this incident is that the runway of Luton airport is in Bedfordshire ~ the exact boundary with Hertfordshire is the end of the runway. So when this particular aircraft "fell off the end of the runway" it fell into Hertfordshire, making it a 'job' for Hitchins crew to deal with. Common sense prevails at incidents such as these and the airport brigade along with the Bedfordshire appliances arrived before Hitchin and extricated the trapped pilot and extinguished the fire. As Luton airport becomes busier and light aircraft travel more popular the likelihood of these incidents grows. Fortunately the above mentioned aircraft is the largest so far experienced to have crashed, excluding the wartime Lancaster, but several light aircraft have crashed in the Breachwood Green area and all have proved fatal to the crews.

L Fm Alex. Armit.

Like "Dantes Inferno" the Cam Gears engineering factory in Wilbury Way continued to have their share of fires and in May a 2000 gallon oil bath caught fire calling for the application of foam from the F.B5X; a foam making branch used in place of the original knapsack type equipment. September saw Rupert Powell a young boy buried in sand at St. Pauls Walden, when a bank collapsed, he was later dug out by the firemen and suffered slight injuries.

1981 saw no fatalities at fires although two firemen were injured in the course of their duties. At a fire in a private house at Grove road Fire man Ron Jack fell through the stairs directly onto the fire that the firemen with their breathing apparatus on the ground floor were searching for. As part of the second "B.A" team he was ordered to search the upstairs rooms and in doing so fell through the stairs, which had been nearly burned through, injuring his back. He was unconscious and had to be pulled out of the smoke filled house by his crew mates. Two dogs were found asphyxiated at this incident.

Fm. Ron Wareham

43

Any animal suffering is distressing to all Firemen, so when they successfully resuscitated Sooty the Cat at a fire in Heathfield road in May 1982, they were justifiably pleased. The same treatment was almost required for Allan Kenyon, when as a remand prisoner at Hitchin Police station he set light to his own bedding in the cell he was locked in. There was only one exit from the cell block and Mr Kenyon was very fortunate that police officers braved the smoke to rescue him before the arrival of the Brigade.

The second accident involving a Fireman occurred on a night "shout" to a fire at the White Horse public house, Tea Green on December 11th. 1981. The weather was cold with compacted snow and ice. The Dodge appliance was stopped by a stranded police car on the long hill up to Pigeon Hill house, subsequently losing its own traction. Whilst the crew pushed the police car up the hill Leading Fireman Bramwell and the driver Fireman Patmore backed the Dodge to the bottom of the hill to have another attempt at the hill. During this process L-Fireman Bramwell attempted to board the moving appliance. Losing his footing on the slippery surface he slid under the vehicle. His leg was broken by the rear wheel of the fire appliance. Ironically the driver, Fireman Patmore was promoted to take Bramwells place during his absence!

Fm Alan Patmore.

The Lea Valley water company mess room in Queen street was gutted by fire in March 1981, and in April at a serious fire in Walsworth road, Steve Stuart jumped from the 2nd floor window of a dwelling house when he found he was trapped by a fire on the ground floor. He landed, uninjured, in a flower bed. At first the firemen did not believe him until they saw the 6"inch impression of his shoes in the flower bed. Guy Grazette also jumped from a lower window and injured his ankle. The cause of the fire: a paraffin heater.

L.Fm Bramwell.

Arson, now, according to the never ending statistics, had increased 5 fold since 1970. There had been 38 cases in 1970; in 1981 it had risen to 263. Also 1 in 4 injuries were caused as the result of fires in the kitchen.

44

After years of purchasing various makes of appliances the Brigade returned to the Dennis Fire "engine co". Hitchin were issued with a brand new DENNIS "R" SERIES which replaced the old 1969 Dennis. The improvements over the 1969 Dennis and even the 1977 Dodge were tremendous. Crew comfort, specially mounted breathing apparatus in the crew seat back rest and high pressure hose reels, to name a few, made this appliance luxurious in comparison. So impressed were the Hitchin Firemen that they volunteered, and were given permission to design the locker stowage, which was subsequently accepted throughout the Brigade, and was even featured in part 5 of the national Fire Brigade manual.

In October 1982 the Piper helpline system was installed in old peoples accomodation within Hitchin. Operated from Peter Sell House in Desborough road it provided immediate contact by the pull of a cord. It was used shortly after installation by Mrs Hayden of West~ -mill Lawns when a dropped cigarette set light to her furniture. The control room immediately called the Brigade. Unfortunately even if teenager Catherine Cliffordhad had this facility she would not have been able to use it as she was already overcome by smoke from the fire which occurred in her flat in Bearton road on the 16th October 1982 at 0136 hours. When the Brigade arrived two breathing apparatus men were sent into the smoke filled first floor with a hose

"Dennis "R" Series"

reel. Catherine was found by Leading Fireman Armit on her bed wrapped in a continental quilt (which it is thought contributed to her survival.) The severity of the fire gave all indications that she was deceased. As the smoke was clearing, Sub officer Dolan went to inspect the room & the body. To his astonishment Catherine moved when touched ~ and then the action really carried rapidly down the stairs by Leading Fireman Tilley & Sub.off: Dolan, with more firemen helping on the way down a forced entry was made to a downstairs flat, where along with approximately 10 Firemen 2 ambulance men with resuscitation equiment the whole lot "placed" Catherine on the bed of the unknown occupant. Not unexpectedly the BED COLLAPSED. Fortunately although Catherine Clifford received serious burns internally and externally, she completely recovered, later married her boyfriend, who had made several attempts to rescue her, and is now a mother. A Christmas card arrives every year at Hitchin Fire Station from the family thanking the Firemen

Catherine Clifford

In December 1982 the Brigade rushed to North Herts Maternity Hospital in Bedford road, to a fire in the boiler house. Further investigation found Customs & Excise officials burning confiscated contraband material including thousands of cigarettes.

45

In 1983 the Hertfordshire Chief Fire Officer Edward Faulkner, "Lashed the County Council", saying, "North Hertfordshire were 42 Firemen under strength and £200000 was required. Hitchin still soldiered on with 12 full time & 6 retained Firemen, to some degree undermining the C.F.O.s argument, and certainly tempting the county council to adopt the day manning duty system as practiced at Hitchin, on more stations throughout Hertfordshire. When costing had been carried out in 1975 it was found that Hitchin with its 18 firemen was rated at half the expense of a full time station.

Animals feature in 1983, in as much as the home of Charles Dickins at Shillington, built in 1522 was saved by "Patch the dog", alerting his owner to a roof fire by barking, and "Gladys the Goose" saved a house in Harkness Way when the roof was struck by lightning. Lightning was again responsible for damage to a house in Bradleys corner. 9 cows were electrocuted in Whitwell when lightning travelled along their wire compound. Initially lightning was blamed for NIRA SAUJANIS burns suffered in the garden of her home in Orchard road during the same storm. There was little the Brigade could do to alleviate her suffering. It later transpired that the 90% burns to her body had been self inflicted. She died three months later in a London hospital.

The Fish 'n' Chicken shop in Hermitage road called the brigade when the oil ignited in the frying ranges. Sub Officer Lemm was slightly burned having tried every extinguishing medium in the book. His breathing apparatus men were so cover-ed in batter that they looked ready for frying themselves. The amount of black smoke issu-ing from the chimney three floors above caused one wag to remark that it was reminiscent of a missippi river boat. The two Hitchin pumps were ordered to 40 Bancroft late one evening in 1983. On arrival it was apparent to the officer in charge, Sub. Officer Dolan, that more than two pumps were required to the conflag--ration that faced them. An area 100 yards by 20 yards and all the small businesses therein was alight. Within these businesses lay the hazards firemen have to contend with~ Paint Solvents, acetylene & oxygen cylinders When one of these cylinders exploded at this fire, the "old hands" hastily disappeared leaving new young retained Fireman ANDREW LEMM standing his ground, fortunately behind a brick wall. Wondering no doubt why he was all alone!

During this incident a horrific accident on the Codicote road in Hitchin when a motorcycle collided with a car, killing the rider & severely injuring the driver. The Baldock retained crew answered this call.

C.F.O. Faulkner
Q.F.S.M.

46

The year 1984 started with a tragedy when 83 year old Geneva Charles died in a fire at her home in Ickleford road. It was believed to have started when burning soot from the chimney fell unnoticed onto the carpet. Mrs Charles tried to escape by the back door but was over come by smoke.

The Hitchin Firemen at this time consisted of several men who had been at the station since it was opened in 1968. This year was to see one of them go. Fireman Arthur Golding suffered a mild heart attack and could no longer undertake full duties. During his last months on "light duties" as a master carpenter he coach built the inside of the newly appointed Hitchin salvage tender.

At 0238 hours on 27th October 1984 the two Hitchin appliances were ordered to 60 KINGS HEDGES, WESTMILL, there to be confronted by a serious house fire in which Victor Piskun

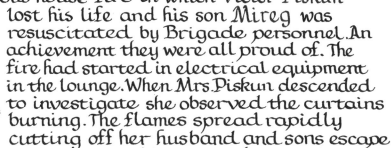

Salvage Unit.

lost his life and his son Mireg was resuscitated by Brigade personnel. An achievement they were all proud of. The fire had started in electrical equipment in the lounge. When Mrs. Piskun descended to investigate she observed the curtains burning. The flames spread rapidly cutting off her husband and sons escape route. Attempts were made by neighbours with a ladder to reach the boys bedroom, when his calls for help were heard. But the fire broke out of the lounge window and started to penetrate the boys bedroom window above. At this time the Brigade arrived. Two firemen in breathing apparatus made their way up the stairs, whilst three more B.A men used a ladder to enter the main bedroom window. The fire in the lounge being dealt with by firemen with hose reels. Victor Piskun was found almost immediately and brought to the ground floor level. His son was found shortly after and successfully resuscitated. The actions of the firemen earned them a commendation from the FIRE & PUBLIC PROTECTION COMM: recommended by the C.F.O and the Divisional Commander, Ronald Ambrose (O/c Hitchin 1968).

The ceremony took place at Hitchin Fire Station in February 1985. Many Councillors, senior officers of the Brigade, the wives and families of the Firemen and local businessmen attended. The crewmen commended were ÷ Sub. Officer Dolan, Leading Firemen Armit & Bramwell, Firemen Patmore, Bateman, Wickham, Jack, Retained Leading Fireman Tilley & Firemen Lemm A.S, Huthwaite. M.

47

The same unselfishness to duty was again shewn at an arson fire in the lift cage at CROFT COURT, Grammar School walk where 13 persons, the majority of whom were elderly were taken out by means of the buildings own fire escapes, the Brigade having made their way up from the 2nd floor through the smoke, checking the landings on the way. Two Firemen, Springett & Brown gave their face masks to two of the elderly people whilst assisting them to safety, an experience the old people thoroughly enjoyed! All persons were safely removed from the incident and on this occasion the arsonist WAS CAUGHT and later imprisoned.

By now Hitchin had two first class appliances, the 1980 Dennis "R" series and an Angloco Shelvoke Automatic carrying the 13·5m ladder. The Dennis was close to the hearts of the Hitchin Firemen as they had designed the locker layout which was standardised and used throughout the Brigade. This was featured in Part 5 of the Brigade manuals. The Shelvoke was designed with a crew survival cab and is an up to the minute appliance.

Fm. Alan Springett

In April 1987 the Brigade celebrated the centenary of the purchase of the St. George steam fire engine. Organised by local teacher and steam enthusiast DEREK WHEELER, with his steam appliance very similar to the St. George, he planned to follow as near as possible the route taken so many years ago. Photographs were later taken by Museum curator ALAN FLECK complete in historical costume outside of the Sun Hotel as T.B.LATCHMORE had done 100 years before. Champagne from the management of the hotel was supplied and then on to the Priory to get the steamer pumping as had happened with the kind permission of Mr Radcliffe 100 years ago. On this occasion the horse pond was used, the property now of the Mutual Assurance, the present owners of the Priory. They also supplied LIQUID refreshments!

In July 1987, another Hitchin resident Mrs Radgah Abra died as a result of a fire at her house in Uplands Avenue. As her husband was being held prisoner by the regime of Col. Gadaffi in Libya her death made national headlines. In October of that year the Hertfordshire Fire Brigade "lost one of their own", when FIREMAN STUART LOUGH and BARRY POMFRET from Hatfield Fire Station (one of Hitchins sister stations) crashed their Dodge emergency rescue tender in Baldock on their way to a road traffic accident. Stuart Lough was killed instantly and Barry Pomfret suffered multiple injuries, he survived. The Hitchin appliance was ordered to this incident, but could do nothing but look on in despair at their dead colleague and the wreckage of the appliance.

Angloco - Shelvoke "Automatic 1984
©.128 C.V.H.

48

When I am called to duty God
Wherever flames may rage
Give me strength to save some Life
Whatever be its age
Help me to embrace a little Child
Before it is to Late
Or save an older Person from the
horror of that fate
Enable me to be alert
hear the weakest shout
quickly and efficiently
Put the fire out
to fill my calling
give the best in me

And...
And...
To put...
And...
To quench
every...
neighbour...
And protect
your will...
Please bless
me Technly,

His property
restoring to
I HAVE to care
my Life
to risk
thank to my
hand, My
dearest my
Wife

Semper Paratus

Following the tragic accident at Baldock, the Hitchin Firemen decided to have a collection for the widow of Fireman Lough and Fireman Pomfret. It was decided that a hand written letter be circulated throughout the shops and industrial premises of Hitchin and that the Brigade would take both appliances into the town centre on the 10th November 1987 and use collecting boxes. The result was magnificent, over £1700 was raised from the letter appeal, all of which went to the FIRE SERVICE NATIONAL BENEVOLENT FUND which cares for the families of injured or deceased Firemen. The towns people of Hitchin have reason to be proud, as in a period of six hours they donated £1395! This was proportionally shared between the two families. Fm. Springett & Sub. Officer Dolan represented Hitchin at the funeral at St Etheldreda Church, Hatfield. As a final token of respect from the Hitchin Firemen an illuminated address of the church service and the 24 Brigades who attended was presented to Hatfield Fire station.

Although this book records the history of the HITCHIN FIRE BRIGADE from its earliest days, the Brigade goes on, answering more calls every year, over 700 in 1987. Ranging from the simple chimney fire to aircraft crashes, & chemical incidents, where the Hitchin firemen undertake decontamination duties, and of course the serious fires and road traffic accidents that regularly occur. In some ways Hitchin is keeping more of its integrity as a towns Brigade than other stations which do not utilise the day manning system. This book is being written in 1988 and personnel are changing. Many of the "Old hands" are retir--ing or are preparing to, leaving the way open for young men to replace them. Some--times coming from far afield, the day --manning duty system necessitates their

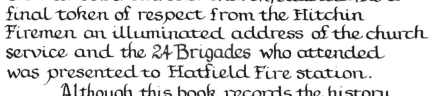

Fire Services National Benevolent Fund.

Fm Cliff Butterworth.   Fm Denzil Codd.

living on the station making them automatically Hitchin residents and putting down "roots". So I hope it will con--tinue, until the time comes when the History of the Hitchin Fire Brigade will be updated. Certainly when that day comes, things will have changed. But when it is considered; the differ--ence in technology between 1834~1988, has not changed the basic roll of the Fireman, to put out fires and be ready when the public calls upon him to do his DUTY.

I am very pleased with the Brigade, I don't think there is another Brigade in the country can touch it. There is not another Brigade with the energy & pluck of our Brigade in London or wher-ever you like"

Charles Loftus Barham. November 5 th: 1920.
Chief Fire Officer; Hitchin Fire Brigade.

The Officers in Charge
Hitchin Fire Brigade

1815 ~ 1851	Supt: I. Newton.
1851 ~ 1866	Supt: W. Jackson.
1866 ~ 1875	Supt: J. Lewin.
1875 ~ 1895	Capt: I. Chalkley.
1895 ~ 1912	Capt: E. Logsdon.
1912 ~ 1922	Capt: C.L. Barham.
1922 ~ 1922	Capt: J.T. Chalkley.
1922 ~ 1922	Capt: A. Foster.
1922 ~ 1926	Capt: J. Davey
1926 ~ 1928	Capt: J. Reynolds.
1928 ~ 1939	Capt: D. Powell.
1939 ~ 1940	C.F.O: Clark.
1940 ~ 1941	C.F.O: Kehoe.
1941 ~ 1946	{ Company Off: Reynolds. Sub. Off: R. French; Company. O. Rogers
1946 ~ 1958 1948 ~ 1956	{ Station Off. R. French. Leading Fm. G. Guyton.
1956 ~ 1958	Leading Fm. C. Preston.
1958 ~ 1961	Leading Fm. T. Sullivan.
1961 ~ 1962	Leading Fm. Robinson.
1963 ~ 1965	Leading Fm. Mann.
1965 ~ 1967	Sub. Off: T. Sullivan.
1967 ~ 1971	Stn: Off: R. Ambrose.
1971 ~ 1973	Stn: Off: H. Wheeler.
1973 ~ 1974	Stn: Off: K. Carbin.
1974 ~ 1976	Sub. Off: T. Sullivan.
1976	Sub. Off: D. Dolan
1976	Sub. Off: A. Lemm.

DEATHS BY FIRE IN THE HITCHIN AREA.

	DATE	NAME	AGE	LOCATION	REASON.
1	22nd March 1853.	Mrs. Gatward		Cock street	Tried to retrieve her jewellery.
2	1917	Elizabeth Chapman	24	Munitions factory	Dress caught fire.
3	1918	Mrs. Osmond (invalid)	31	53 Kings road	Fell into domestic fire.
4	1920	Sarah Cotton ~"~	77	52 Ickleford road.	Overcome by smoke.
6	1954	Brian Davies	18	Wilshere crescent.	Trapped by m/cycle which caught fire.
5	1940	James Tomlin	73	Russell Slip	Fell into domestic fire.
7	1941	Colin Sparkhill	5½	Westmill road	Burned by ~" — "~
8	1956	Mary Ann Brown	3½	Mattocke road	Dress caught fire, dancing in front of fire.
9	1962	Ada Whyberd	67	Highover Way	Overcome by smoke.
10	1963	Carolyn Denne		Willian road	Dressing gown caught fire.
11	1967	Cardela French	83		Night dress caught fire
12	1970	Ada McKenzie	82	High Dane	Dressing gown caught fire.
13	1970	Henrietta Worledge	87	Chesnut row, Lilley.	Overcome by smoke.
14	1971	Anthony Smith	44	Basildon, Essex.	Trapped in blazing petrol tanker
15	1975	Victor Page	29	Northants	Burned to death in motor car at Lt. Wymondley following road traffic acc:
16		William Hogarth	39	Norwich	
17		Alan Stevens	20	Aberdeen	
19	1977	Arthur Maurice	45	Fox P.H. Darley Hall.	Severe burns.
18	1976	Jessica Allcock	89	Austage end.	Burned to death.
20	1978	Fatima Khatoon	1½	York road	Overcome by smoke.
21	1979	Beatrice Rowe Gillett	72	Salusbury Lane, Offley	Burned in bed
22	1979	Eliza: Danahar	68	Chaucer Way	Overcome by smoke.
23	1983	Nija Saujani	28	Orchard road	Died due to burns (3 months) later.
25	1984	Victor Piscun	30	Kings Hedges	Overcome by smoke.
24	1984	Emma Charles	83	Ickleford road	" " "
26	1987	Radislava Abra	54	Uplands Avenue.	suffered heart attack after fighting fire.

Hitchin Firemen
1814 - 1988

Abbiss.F.	Clinton.G.	Golby.	Latchmore.J.	Parr.	Spencer.
Abbiss.J.	Clouting.J.	Golding.A.	Latchmore.B.	Parker.S.	Stevens.
Allen.P.	Coleman.H.	Goodman.	Lee.A.	Parfitt.	Stapleton.K.
Aland.T.	Copely.G.	Gilham.	Lemm.A.	Perks.C.	Sullivan.T.
Allingham.R.	Cooper W.	Grant.W.	Lemm.D	Peploe.	Sweetman.W.
Ambrose.R.	Cooper.	Grant.D.	Lemm.A.S.	Petridge.	Symons.F.
Appleby.W.	Cook.W.	Grant.F.	Lemon.P.	Pickering.	Taylor.J.
Alston.B.	Codd.D.	Grellett.	Lewin.A.	Powell.D.	Thair.E.
Armit.A.	Condor.A.	Green.A.	Lewin.J.	Preston.C.	Terry.H.
Avery.J.	Coulson.	Green.A.J.	Lloyd.E.	Prime.	Theobald.
Ayloth.A.	Crees.A.	Green.C.	Logsdon.E	Pryor.E.	Thomas.W.
Bailey.I.	Croft.	Griffin.	Logsdon.jnr.	Purdy.H.	Throssell.A.
Baker.A.	Crosier	Grimes.	Lockwood	Ramsden.W.	Tilley.L.
Barham.A.	Crouch	Grice.	Lovatt.	Rainbow.	Tomlin.R.
Barham.H.	Cutler.R.	Gray.F.	Lyle.G.	Read.	Turner
Barham.C.L	Davey.J.	Guyton.G.	Males.	Reed.A.	Trigg.H.
Barham.C.L.jnr	Davey.S.	Hagger.D.	Mason.	Reynolds.J	Underwood.
Barrel.H	Davis.C.	Hair.J.	Maidment.E.	Reynolds.E.	Uridge.
Bateman.L.	Davis.	Hailey.G.	Marshall.D.	Reynolds.T.	Upchurch.
Bell.J.	Davies.A.	Hall.T.	Major.D.	Reynolds.I.	Valentine.
Bavister.M.	Dennis.	Harrison.	Matthews.C	Rogers.	Vickers.S.
Bennett.J.	Denton.H.	Hawkins.	Mills.J.	Robinson.	Whatson.F.
Best.G.	Dickenson.	Heron.S.	Miller.D.	Rudd	Wooding.
Bramwell.T.	Dockree.P.	Harding	Miller.	Russell.A.	Webb.E
Brazier.G.	Dolan.D.	Holiday.	Merrick.	Rutland.A	Warren.J.
Barker.M.	Donovan.	Hill.W.	Morgan.R.	Sale.H.	Whittles.
Brooker	Eldred.H.	Hilton.G.	Moore.	Sanders.F.	Wiggs.
Brown.G.	Ellard.J.	Howard.W.	Morgan.	Savage.P.	Warrington.
Bromfield	Ellis.D.	Howard.D.	Morriss.O.	Seymour.A.	Waldock.J.
Bullen.M.	Elliss	Hull.	Moul.	Seymour.F.	Woods.P.
Burton.T.	Enoch.N.	Hunter.	Mustoe.H	Simpson.D.	Waters.A.
Butterworth.C.	Fairey.G.	Huthwaite.D.	Muncey.R.	Sell.	Watson.H
Cannon.A.	Fisher.	Huthwaite.P.	Napier.M.	Sibley.W.	Waldon.
Cannon.Ha.	Foster.A.	Huthwaite.M.	Newton.I.	Shakesby.	Wright.E.
Cannon.Hu.	Foster	Hammond.A.	Newton.C.	Shambrook.	Waller.H.
Cannon.C.	Fraser	Jack.R.	Nixon.R.	Shillitoe.S.	Watson.J.W.
Carbin.K.	French.C.	Jackson.W.	North.J.	Scott.A.	Williams.
Cartwright.	French.R.	Jeaves.	North.J.G.	Skelcher.	Whittenbury.A.
Chard.J.	Froy.	Johnson.R.	Norris.H	Slater.C.	Wakefield.E.
Chalkley.I	Garrett.E.	Joyner.J.	Oakman.J.	Slater.	West.
Chalkley.J.T.	Garrett.L	Kehoe.	O'Dell.J.	Smith.R	Walters.M.
Cain.J.	Garrett.J.	King.C.	Oliver.	Smith.L.	Walton.
Chamberlain	Garvie.	King.A.	Osborne.	Smith.	Wareham.R.
Cheverton.C.	Gatward.J.	Kitchener.J.	Orvis.S.	Smallwood	Wickham.D.
Clark.R.	Gatward.W.	Kitely.J.	Pack.J.	Spencer.	Wheeler.H.
Clark.G	Goddard.F.	Lane.	Pack.G.	Springett.S.	Wilson.
Clark.	Goddard.N.	Langford	Parker.S	Springett.A.	Willis.J
Chapman	Goldsmith.J.	Langford.A.	Patmore.A	Stallabrass.	Webb.
Circuit.P	Crozier*	Bucket.M.*	Wise*		

* Female A.F.S. Staff World War II